Pure Vegetarian Delights

Published by :
Lotus Press Publishers & Distributors

Pure Vegetarian Delights

Aruna Anand

Lotus PRESS

4735/22, Prakash Deep Building
Ansari Road, Darya Ganj,
New Delhi - 110002

Lotus Press : Publishers & Distributors
Unit No. 220, 2nd Floor, 4735/22, Prakash Deep Building,
Ansari Road, Darya Ganj, New Delhi- 110002
Ph.: 41325510, 98118-38000
• E-mail : lotuspress1984@gmail.com
www.lotuspress.co.in

Pure Vegetarian Delights

ISBN: 81-8382-091-3

Printed & Published by : **Lotus Press Publisher & Distributors,** New Delhi-02

INTRODUCTION

You will find it simple to plan a complete exciting meal from any of the tested recipes in this book. You can choose from a wide variety of tasty pure vegetarian Indian dishes. For special occasions surprise your family with any of the delicious festival dishes of India.

Some recipes have variations, and you can always invent your own recipes with your personal touch. You will soon discover that you can cook many more dishes in addition to the recipes given in this book.

Special care has been taken to give the most authentic recipes and the most common ones, in the most simple terms.

GLOSSARY OF INGREDIENTS

English	Hindi
Condiments and Nuts	
Almonds	Badam
Aniseed	Saunf
Arrowroot	Ararot
Asafoetida	Heeng
Bay leaf	Tej patta
Peppercorns	Kali mirch
Caraway	Shahijeera
Cardamoms	Elaichi
Cashewnuts	Kaju
Cinnamon	Dalchini
Cloves	Laung
Coconut	Narial
Coriander	Dhania
Cumin	Jeera
Curry leaves	Kadi patta
Dry ginger	Sonth
Fenugreek	Methi
Garlic	Lahsun
Ginger	Adrak
Jaggery	Gur
Nutmeg	Jaiphal
Peanuts	Moongphali
Poppy seeds	Khus-khus
Raisins	Kishmish
Red chillies	Lal mirch
Saffron	Kesar
Sesame	Til
Tamarind	Imli
Turmeric	Haldi
Vinegar	Sirka
Fennel	Ajwain
Vegetables	
Beetroot	Chukundar
Bittergourd	Karela
Brinjal	Baingan
Cabbage	Bandh gobhi
Capsicum	Shimla mirch
Carrot	Gajar
Cauliflower	Phool gobhi
Celery	Ajwain ka patta
Colocasia	Arbi ka Patta

English	Hindi
leaves	
Coriander leaves	Hari dhaniya
Cucumber	Kheera
Lady'sfinger	Bhindi
Mint	Pudina
Mushrooms	Kukar moote
Onion	Pyaz
Peas	Matar
Potatoes	Aloo
Pumpkin	Kaddu
Spinach	Palak
Bottlegourd	Lauki
Spring onion	Hari pyaz
Tomato	Tamatar

Cereals and Lentils

English	Hindi
Bengal gram	Chana dal
Black gram	Urad dal
Gram flour	Besan
Corn	Makai
Cornflour	Makai ka atta
Fried gram	Bhuna chana
Lentil	Masoor dal
Green gram	Moong dal
Semolina	Sooji
Red gram	Arhar dal
Vermicelli	Sevian

Fruits

English	Hindi
Apples	Seb
Apricots	Khubani
Banana	Kela
Fig	Anjeer
Grapes	Angoor
Mango	Aam
Orange	Santra
Papaya	Papita
Peaches	Aadu
Peas	Nashpati
Pineapple	Ananas

GLOSSARY OF COOKING TERMS

Batter: A mixture of flour and besan flour, a variety of other ingredients and liquid of such consistency that it can be beaten or stirred, used generally to coat foods for frying, or for making idlis and such like delicacies.

Beat: To mix ingredients together with a circular up and down motion using a whisk, spoon or an electric beater.

Blend: To stir, rather than beat, ingredients until they are thoroughly combined.

Chop: To cut into small pieces.

Crush: To pulverise by rolling with a rolling pin or by mashing until the food is of coarse powder.

Dice: To cut into small cubes.

Fry: To cook in hot fat or oil.

Garnish: To decorate a dish by adding other foodstuffs over the main dish.

Grate: To reduce food like some vegetables or cheese by rubbing them on sharp cutting teeth of a grater.

Grease: To rub fat or oil on the surface of vessels.

Knead: To work dough by pressing it with the heels of the hands, folding and turning it and pressing it until it has been worked into a contained elastic texture.

Mash: To soften and breakdown food by using the hands or masher or the back of a spoon.

Mayonnaise: A thick sauce made of flour, oil, vinegar mustard powder.

Melt: To change fat and solid dissolvable foods into a liquid state by heating.

Season: To add salt, spices or other ingredients in hot oil to increase the flavours of food.

Shred: Cut in fine strips.

Simmer: To cook a liquid barely at the boiling point. The surface will show only a few bubbles breaking slowly.

CONTENTS

SOUPS

SOUPS

1. PUMPKIN SOUP

Ingredients

20 ml olive oil
2 tbsps chopped celery
2 bay leaves
5 fresh peppercorns
20 ml white wine
20 ml fresh cream
¼ tsp ground pepper
5 tbsps chopped onions
2 tbsps chopped garlic
200 gms red pumpkin cleaned and diced
salt to taste
4 cups vegetables stock

For the Garnish

20 ml olive oil
4 tsps fresh cream

Method

Heat the oil in a heavy-bottomed pan. Add the onion, celery, garlic and bay leaves, and sauté till the onions are light brown in colour. Add the diced pumpkin and fresh peppercorns, and sauté till the vegetables are soft. Season with salt. Add the white wine and vegetable stock and cook for a further 25 minutes till the pumpkin is soft and pulpy. Remove from heat and puree till the soup is of a smooth consistency. Return to the heat, add the fresh cream and pepper powder, and simmer it for a further five minutes. Serve hot, garnished with a dash of olive oil and a swirl of fresh cream.

2. LENTIL SOUP

Ingredients

- ½ cup lentils
- 1 tbsp vegetable oil
- ½ tsp mustard
- a pinch of hing
- 2 tbsps chopped vegetables
- 1 cup onion, chopped
- 1 medium tomato, chopped
- 2 tbsps chopped coriander leaves
- 1 tbsp coconut milk
- 1 tsp salt
- ½ tsp cumin
- ½ tsp sesame seeds
- 4-5 bay leaves
- ½ clove garlic, chopped
- 1 tbsp brown sugar
- ½ tsp cumin-coriander powder
- ½ tsp garam masala
- 1 tsp pepper powder

Method

Cook the lentils in 2 cups water until soft. Puree it, add the salt and mix well. Heat oil in a saucepan. Add cumin, mustard, hing and sesame, and let them splutter. Add the garlic, onion, tomato and sauté till the tomato is soft. Add the brown sugar and vegetables and sauté till the vegetables are cooked but crisp. Add the powdered spices and garam masala. Stir–fry for half a minute. Add the lentil mixture and a cup of water, and cook until the ingredients are well blended. Decorate with coriander leaves, and serve hot.

3. PEANUT SOUP

Ingedients

- 1 cup roasted peanuts, crushed coarsely
- 1 tsp pepper powder
- 1 tsp salt
- 2 tbsps chopped coriander leaves
- a pinch of asafoetida
- 1 tbsp cumin-coriander powder
- 1 tsp turmeric powder
- ½ tsp garam masala
- 1 tbsp vegetable oil
- 1 tsp cumin-mustard seeds

Method

Mix together the peanuts, cumin-coriander powder, pepper powder, turmeric powder, turmeric powder, salt, garam masala with 3 cups water. Heat oil in a saucepan, add the asafoetida, mustard and cumin. When they splutter, add the peanut mixture. Bring to a boil, remove from heat and serve hot, garnished with coriander leaves.

4.YOGHURT SOUP

Ingredients

- 1½ cups plain yoghurt
- ¾ tsp ginger powder
- 2½ cups water
- ½ tsp mustard
- ½ tsp fenugreek seeds
- 1 tsp chopped coriander leaves
- 1 ½ tbsps besan flour
- 1 ½ tsps salt
- 1 ½ tsps ghee (or butter)
- 3-4 bay leaves
- ½ tsp turmeric powder

Method

With an egg beater, mix well the yoghurt, besan flour and ginger powder. Add the salt and water. Heat ghee in a saucepan. Splutter the mustard, add the bay leaves, fenugreek and turmeric. Then add the youghurt mixture, stirring constantly while heating the soup. When it comes to a boil, remove and serve hot, garnished with coriander.

5. CHILLED CUCUMBER SOUP

Ingredients

- ½ piece ginger grated
- 2-3 cups water
- 1 sprig finely chopped mint
- salt and pepper to taste
- 1-2 slices bread
- 1 small green chilli
- 2-3 tbsps cream, whipped smooth
- 1 tsp sugar

Method

Chop the cucumber into large chunks, and boil in water. Cool and blend in a mixie along with bread, ginger and green chilli. Sieve. Add the sugar, salt and pepper. Chill for two hours. While serving, pour into individual bowls. Carefully pour a swirl of cream, spinkle with chopped mint.

6. CAULIFLOWER-BROCCOLI SOUP

Ingredients

500 gms broccoli, cut into florets
1 medium onion, chopped
2 small stalks celery,
1 clove garlic, crushed
1 medium potato, peeled and chopped
4-5 mint leaves finely chopped
250 gms cauliflower, cut into florets
¼ tsp dried and crushed herbs (optional)
2 cups skimmed milk
1 tsp butter
pepper to taste
salt to taste

Method

Heat butter in a saucepan. Add the garlic and onion, stir-fry till soft. Add the water, potato, celery, broccoli and cauliflower. Bring to a boil. Reduce heat and simmer till potato is soft. Add the herb. Puree the mixture. Boil again till the mixture is thickened. Add salt, pepper, mint and milk. Serve hot with soup sticks and butter.

7. HOT AND SOUR SOUP

Ingredients

2 tbsps finely shredded cabbage
1 small stalk celery, finely
2 tbsps finely slivered carrot
1 tbsp finely chopped

chopped
1 tbsp finely chopped cauliflower
¼ tsp grated ginger
1 tsp brown vinegar
salt to taste
spring onions
½ tsp red chilli sauce
¼ tsp pepper powder
2 tsps cornflour
4 cups water
1 tsp butter or oil

Method

Heat the butter, add the vegetables and ginger, except the onions, stir–fry till cooked, add the spring onions, and stir. Add water, chilli sauce, soya sauce, vinegar and stir. Bring to a boil and simmer for 7-8 minutes. Add the salt and pepper. Mix cornflour in ½ cup water, and pour into soup, stirring continuously; cook for two minutes. Serve hot.

8. GINGER SOUP

Ingredients

50 gms cabbage, shredded
50 gms carrots, chopped
1 capsicum, chopped
20 gms ginger, julienned
salt and pepper to taste
1 tsp oil
1 lt water
10 gms cornflower
1 tsp soya sauce
1 tsp vinegar
10 gms garlic, cruched
a pinch of ajinomoto
1 spring onion, chopped
2 sprigs coriander leaves, finely chopped

Method

Heat the oil, and add the ginger and garlic. Sauté it for half a minute. Add the chopped vegetables and stir-fry. Add the water and when it boils, add the soya sauce, vinegar, ajinomoto and coriander. After a minute, add the cornflour paste. Add the spring onion. Boil for a minute. Serve hot.

9. MIXED BEAN SOUP

Ingredients

½ cup black beans
½ cup green lentils
2 tsps lemon juice
½ chopped capsicum
½ chopped garlic
½ tsp oil
2 cloves
salt and pepper to taste
6-8 croutons
¼ cup kidney beans
½ cup chopped spring onions
½ cup, chopped tomatoes
¼ tsp turmeric powder
2" stick cinnamon
2 tsps chopper coriander leaves

Method

Pressure cook the beans and lentils with turmeric powder, cloves and cinnamon. Heat the oil in a pan. Saute the spring onions and garlic. When the onion is brown, add the capsicum and tomatoes, and sauté well, lower the heat, and let the vegetables cook. Add the cooked beans-lentils mixture, discarding the cloves and cinnamon. If the soup is too thick, add more hot water. Add the salt, lemon juice and pepper. Remove from heat. Serve hot garnished with coriander and croutons.

10. BABY CORN SOUP

Ingredients

5 baby corns, grated and pressure cooked
1 medium onion, chopped
salt to taste
1 small cup mixed vegetables, boiled
1 cup milk
1 clove garlic
pepper powder to taste
1 tbsp butter

Method

Heat the butter and fry the onions. Mash the baby corn, add this to the fried onions. Add the boiled vegetables, salt and pepper, and heat till all the ingredients blend well. Garnish with grated cheese and coriander leaves.

11. CHEESE SOUP

Ingredients

- 1 cup cottage cheese, cubed
- 1 tsp ginger-garlics paste
- 1 tsp cornflour
- 2 cups tomato sauce
- 1 cup vegetables, chopped finely
- 14 tsp turmeric powder
- mint leaves for garnishing
- 5 tomatoes, chopped finely
- 1 tpsp oil
- ½ tsp garam masala powder
- ½ tsp chilli powder
- salt to taste

Method

Fry the cheese and keep aside. Add.the onions in the same oil and sauté till onions turn pink. Add the cornflour and stir-fry for a few seconds. Add the tomatoes, ginger-garlic paste, chilli powder, turmeric powder and garam masala. Stir-fry for a minute. Add three cups of water and simmer for 15 minutes after adding the salt. Cool and puree. Strain the mixture. Add the vegetables to the mixture and simmer till vegetables are cooked and soft. Add the tomato sauce and mix well. Add the fried cheese to this and serve hot, garnished with mint leaves.

12. MEXICAN SOUP

Ingredients

1 kg tomatoes
2 potatoes, cut into small pieces
2 curry leaves
1 tbsp cornflour
salt and pepper to taste
3 onions, cut long
4 tsps grated ginger
2 cloves, powdered
8 cups water
1 tbsp oil

Method

Mix all the ingredients except cornflour and oil. Pressure cook for 15 minutes. Heat the oil in a pan, and roast the cornflour. Add the mixture from the pressure cooker. Cook for 5-7 minutes. Garnish with butter, and serve hot.

13. HOT NOODLE SOUP

Ingredients

¾ cup boiled noodles
½ tsp sugar
½ tsp pepper powder
½ tsp ajinomoto
1 tsp salt
½ tsp soya sauce
2 tsps cornflour, mixed in ¼ cup water

For the vegetable stock

1 onion, chopped
2 cups cabbage, shredded
½ tsp chopped ginger
½ tsp chopped garlic
½ tsp salt
1 carrot, chopped
7 cups water
1 potato, chopped
4-5 french beans, chopped

Method

Put all the ingredients for the vegetable stock in a cooker and pressure cook them. Strain and use the liquid for the soup.

Add to it the pepper, sugar, soya sauce and ajinomoto. Boil, then mix the cornflour paste to it, stirring continuously. Add the vegetables that were pressure cooked. Simmer for 2-3 minutes. Add the boiled noodles, and serve hot.

14. MUSHROOM SOUP

Ingredients

200 gms mushrooms, quartered
300 ml milk
2 bay leaves
4 cloves
1 tbsp cornflour
¼ tsp pepper powder
2 medium sized onions, chopped
5-6 peppercorns
2 tbsps butter
salt to taste
a pinch of nutmeg powder

Method

Boil the milk along with the bay leaves, peppercorns and cloves. Strain and keep the milk. Melt the butter in a saucepan. Add the onions and mushrooms, and cook till they are soft. Add the flour and sauté till there is no raw flavour coming form the flour, taking care that the flour does not get burnt. Pour the milk slowly, and stir continuously to avoid lumps from forming. Cook for five minutes. Puree the mixture when cool. Boil it, correct the consistency by adding more milk if required. Add the cream, salt, pepper and nutmeg powders. Stir well, and serve hot with a dash of cream.

15. CARROT SOUP

Ingredients

1 tomato, chopped
2 cups skimmed milk
salt and sugar to taste
4 carrots, chopped
½ tsp pepper powder

Method

Boil water in a pan. Lower the heat and add the vegetables. Cook till tender. Add the pepper. Puree the mixture, adding the milk, salt and sugar. Strain and chill. Serve cool, garnished with slivered almonds.

16. MIXED VEGETABLES SOUP

Ingredients

100 gms potatoes, chopped
100 gms onions, chopped
100 gms turnip, chopped
1 tbsp butter
1 tsp ginger-garlic paste
8 cups water
100 gms carrots, chopped
100 gms peas
2-3 bay leaves
5-6 black peppercorns
salt to taste

Method

Heat the butter in a pan. Fry the bay leaves, ginger-garlic paste, pepper and salt for half a minute. Add all the vegetables and sauté for five minutes. Add the water and pressure cook this mixture. Serve hot.

17. POTATO-ONION SOUP

Ingredients

3 medium-sized potatoes, cut into large chumks
1 tbsp butter
2 tbsps lemon juice
½ tsp pepper powder
2 cups water
salt to taste
1 medium-sized onion, cut into large chunks
¼ cup tomato puree
½ tsp chilli powder
½ tbsp cornflour
1 tbsp chopped coriander leaves

Method

Cook together the potatoes and onions till soft. Puree this and add to it the tomato puree. Blend once. Heat the butter in a pan. Add the chilli and pepper powders and salt. Add the puree and lemon juice and bring to a boil. Reduce the heat. Gradually add the cornflour dissolved in water, and stir continuously when the soup is thick. Serve hot garnished with coriander leaves.

18. SPINACH SOUP

Ingredients

- 3 cups chopped spinach
- 3 ½ cups water
- ½ tsp pepper powder
- ½ tsp cumin powder
- 2 tbsps lemon juice
- 1 cup chopped cucumber
- 1 tbsp butter
- ½ tsp ginger paste
- salt to taste

Method

Put the spinach and cucumber in a saucepan along with water. Cook until tender. Blend in a mixie to a smooth consistency. Heat the butter in a pan. Add the pepper and cumin powder, ginger paste and salt. Add the pureed vegetables and lemon juice. Cook on medium heat for five minutes. Serve hot.

19. SIMPLE TOMATO SOUP

Ingredients

- 2 big tomatoes, halved
- 1 small piece ginger, grated
- coriander leaves for garnishing
- 1 big onion, quartered
- salt and pepper to taste
- 4 cups water

Method

Boil the water. Add the tomatoes and onion pieces, and ginger. Boil for two minutes. Allow to cool. Remove the outer skin of the tomatoes. Puree the mixture. Reheat, adding water if it is too thick. Add the pepper and salt. Serve hot, garnished with chopped coriander leaves.

20. SWEET CORN SOUP

Ingredients

6 large corncobs
2 tbsps cornflour
1 tsp soya sauce
1 tsp vinegar
6 cups water
1 ½ tbsps sugar
1 tsp chilli sauce
salt to taste

Method

Pressure cook the corn kernels till tender. Keep aside ¼ cup cooked kernel. Puree the rest. Cook it in a pan on medium heat. Mix cornflour in 4 tbsps water and add to the boiling mixture. Stir continuously. Add the sugar, salt, sauces, and vinegar. Serve hot, garnished with the boiled corn that has been kept aside.

21. MINESTRONE SOUP

Ingredients

115 gms carrots, diced
115 gms tomatoes, chopped
30 gms grated cheese
15 gms butter
salt to taste
50 gms macaroni
1 tbsp cornflour
115 gms onions, chopped
150 gms peas
2 flakes garlic, chopped
15 gms oil
6½ cups water
1 spring parsley, chopped finely

Method

Heat the oil in a pan, and fry the onions, garlic and parsley. Add all the vegetables. Sauté for a minute. Add the water. Pressure cook this till the vegetables are soft. Add the macaroni, and pressure cook for five minutes. Serve hot, garnished with grated cheese and butter.

SALADS

SALADS

1. MANGO AND POMEGRANATE SALAD

Ingredients

3 ripe mangoes, cubed
1 cucumber chopped
1 capsicum, cut and chaffed
½ cup grapes
2 pomegranates, deseeded
1 medium orange, peeled and segmented

For the Dressing

4 tsps lemon juice
1 tsp pepper powder
1 tsp honey
salt to taste

For the Garnish

2 spring onions, finely chopped

Method

In a bowl, mix the mango cubes, pomegranate seeds, cucumber and capsicum pieces, grapes and orange segments. In another bowl, mix the lemon juice, honey, pepper powder and salt. Pour over the salad, garnish with the spring onions.

2. CHRISTMAS SALAD

Ingredients

50 gms iceberg lettuce
50 gms pomegranate seeds
20 gms garlic flakes, diced
10 olives, sliced
salt and pepper to taste
50 gms carrots, diced
50 gms diced water chestnuts (singhada)
1 tsp chopped parsley
3 cherry tomatoes, halved

To Serve

Lettuce leaves
Green grapes, a handful

Method

In a mixing bowl, mix together all the salad ingredients. Lay a bed of lettuce leaves on a decorative salad platter. Arrange the salad on this, and garnish with the grapes.

3. INDONESIAN SALAD

Ingredients

150 gms cabbage, shredded
150 gms baby corn, cut into small pieces
2 potatoes, boiled and cubed
100 gms carrots, boiled and diced
a bunch of spinach, chopped
200 gms beam sprouts
2 eggs, boiled and halved
150 gms French beans, chopped

For the Dressing

1 tsp olive oil
1 cup peanut butter
1 tsp chilli sauce
2-3 cloves garlic
1 tbsp soya sauce
½ tbsps crushed peanuts

Method

Blanch all the vegetables. Set aside. Heat the oil in a pan and sauté the garlic. Add the peanut butter, soya, chilli sauce, chilli flakes and crushed peanuts. Simmer for about three to four minutes. Remove and set aside. Arrange the vegetables as per your choice and serve with the dressing.

4. CABBAGE SALAD

Ingredients

1 cup shredded cabbage
1 tsp vegetable oil
a pinch of garam masala
juice of half lime
½ tbsp chopped coriander leaves
a pinch of salt
pepper powder to taste

Method

Mix all the ingredients in a bowl. You can either mix the coriander leaves with the ingredients or use it as a garnish.

5.LAYERED SALAD

Ingredients

1 large cucumber, grated in a large-holed grater
1 large tomato, chopped finely
1 bunch lettuce or salad leaves
1 small beetroot
juice of 1 lemon
salt, pepper, sugar to taste
1 large carrot, grated
1 large onion, chopped finely
1 bunch spring onion, chopped
1 small leafy green cabbage

Method

Steam beetroot in a pressure cooker. Peel and slice into thin rounds. Chill all the ingredients separately till crisp. Rinse a transparent glass bowl with cold water. Stick the beetroot slices around the inner wall of the bowl evenly. Spread the tomatoes at the bottom of the bowl. Sprinkle salt and pepper. Spread the spring onions over the tomatoes. Repeat for each vegetable in the following order: cabbage, salad leaves, onion and carrot. Sprinkle lemon juice. Chill before serving.

6. NOODLE SALAD

Ingredients

- 1 cup Maggi noodles, crushed
- 1 onion, chopped
- 1 tbsp finely chopped coriander leaves
- 1 small green chilli, finely chopped
- ¼ tsp chaat masala
- ½ tsp cumin, crushed
- salt to taste
- 1 cucumber, chopped into medium pieces
- 1 stalk mint leaves, finely chopped
- 1 small flake garlic, finely chopped
- 2 pinches black salt
- ½ tsp sugar, powdered

Method

Dry roast the noodles in a heavy pan till light and off white. Stir continuously while roasting. Cool and chill cucumber and tomato, in a large bowl add all the ingredients, except coriander and noodles. Toss with fork till well blended. Add the noodles and toss gently. Garnish with coriander before serving chilled.

7. JELLY SALAD

Ingredients

- 1 packet jelly (set as per instructions)
- 1 large cucumber, diced
- 1 medium apple, diced
- 1 bunch lettuce, shredded
- ¼ medium cabbage, shredded
- 2 slices pineapple, chopped
- 1 carrot, grated

2 tbsps curds
pepper powder to taste
salt to taste
2 tbsps cream
1 tsp sugar

Method

Whip together cream, curds and sugar. Toss all the ingredients, except the jelly and cream-curd mixture. Chill in a large glass bowl. Just before serving, chop the jelly into inch-sized cubes. Mix them in the salad and toss lightly. Pour the whipped cream-curd mixture on the salad and serve immediately.

8. FRUITY SPROUT SALAD

Ingredients

1 cup moong sprouts
1 sweet lime, segmented, peeled and deseeded
6 fresh ripe figs, chopped into quarters
2 oranges, segmented, peeled and deseeded
1 apple, chilled and chopped
2-3 salad leaves, chopped coarsely

For the Dressing

1 tbsp lemon juice
1 tsp honey
salt to taste
1 tsp vinegar
¼ tsp pepper powder

Method

Put all the fruits in a large bowl. Add the sprouts and salad leaves. Mix the ingredients for the dressing thoroughly. Chill it, as also the salad bowl. Before serving, pour dressing over the salad. Mix and toss gently with fork. Serve chilled.

9. MOONG-POMEGRANATE SALAD

Ingredients

1 cup pomegranate seeds
1 cup grated coconut
1 cup moong sprouts
4 red chillies

a pinch of asafoetida
1 tbsp oil
salt to taste
few curry leaves
½ tsp mustard
1 tsp lemon juice

Method

Mix together pomegranate, moong sprouts and coconut. Add the salt and lemon juice and mix well. Heat the oil, add the mustard chillies, asafoetida and curry leaves. Season the salad. Use the coriander for garnishing. For variation you can add finely chopped cucumber, grated ginger or finely chopped green chillies.

10. CORN SALAD

Ingredients

1 cup frozen corn
1 tsp lemon juice
salt to taste
1 tsp olive oil
2 tsps pepper powder

Method

Pressure cook or microwave the corn till done. Add all the other ingredients and serve chilled. Garnish with coriander leaves.

11. GREEN SALAD

Ingredients

2 cups cottage cheese, grated
1 small cucumber, chopped
½ cup chopped tomatoes
2 tsps lemon juice
¼ cup button mushrooms, chopped
¼ cup chopped coriander-mint leaves
5 cabbage leaves, chopped
¼ cup chopped onions
1 green chilli, chopped
¼ cup green peas, boiled
3 tsps grated cheese
salt and pepper to taste

Method

Mix together all the ingredients in a bowl. Add the seasoning and lemon juice, and chill. Serve with grated cheese and chopped leaves.

12. MACARONI-MINT SALAD

Ingredients

- 1 cup macaroni, boiled with salt
- 2 tbsps chopped mint leaves
- salt to taste
- 1 cup pineapple cubes
- ¾ cup chopped tomato
- 3 tbsps shredded lettuce
- 1 tsp lemon juice

Method

Strain the boiled macaroni. Add the other ingredients and mix well. Chill and serve.

13. LOW CALORIE SALAD

Ingredients

- 4 apples, chopped
- 1 orange, peeled, segmented deseeded
- 4 carrots, grated
- ½ cucumber, grated
- 1 pear, chopped
- 1 capsicum, chopped
- 4 sticks celery, chopped
- a few raisins
- ½ cup curds, chilled

Method

Mix all the ingredients in a glass bowl and chill. Before serving, scoop teaspoons of curd on top of the salad and serve chilled.

14. CHANA-CHEESE SALAD

Ingredients

- 2 cups kabuli chana, boiled
- 150 gms cottage cheese (paneer)
- 2 potatoes, boiled and chopped

1 onion, finely chopped
1 bunch coriander leaves, finely chopped
salt to taste
½ tsp chilli powder
juice of 1 lemon
2 firm tomatoes, finely chopped
2 green chillies, finely chopped
1 tsp chaat masala

Method

Cube the cottage cheese into small pieces. In a large salad bowl, add the chana, potatoes, onions, tomatoes, cheese and green chilies. Add all the other ingredients, mix well and chill for a couple of hours before serving.

15. SALAD WITH BAKED APPLES

Ingredients

2 tbsps honey
50 gms peanuts
½ lemon juice
600 gms apples, baked

Method

Skin the baked apples and grate them roughly. Put into a small china bowl. Add honey and lemon juice. Sprinkle with crushed peanuts. Let it rest for an hour. Drizzle whipped cream over it.

16. RAW MANGO-PINEAPPLE SALAD

Ingredients

½ unripe green mango, grated
2 tbsps sprouted moong
1 tbsp freshly grate coconut (optional)
1 green chilli, finely chopped
1 cucumber, grated with its skin
½ juice pineapple
salt to taste
coriander leaves, finely chopped

Method

Mix together all the ingredients. Chill before serving.

CHUTNEYS, SAUCES AND RAITAS

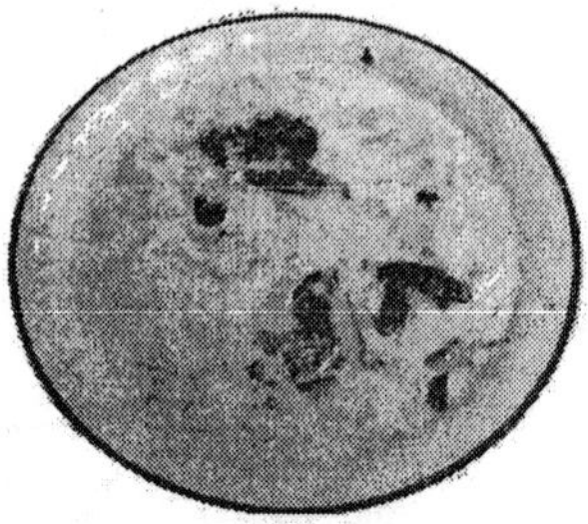

CALORIE FREE
Alfredo
CALORIE FREE
Scampi
CALORIE FREE

CHUTNEYS, SAUCES AND RAITAS

1. ONION CHUTNEY

Ingredients

- 4 onions, chopped into slices
- 2 tbsps coconut scrapings
- 1½ tbsps roasted gram
- 8 red chillies
- salt to taste

Method

Grind the coconut, chillies and roasted gram with salt to a fine paste. Add the onions and grind coarsely.

2. BRINJAL CHUTNEY

Ingredients

- 1 large round brinjal, boiled and mashed
- 2 tsps tamarind extract
- 1 tsp black gram
- a pinch of jaggery
- salt to taste
- 2 green chillies, chopped
- 1 tsp chilli powder
- a pinch of asafoetida
- 1 tbsp oil

Method

In the hot oil, fry the black gram, asafoetida and chilli. Grind this with the tamarind extract. Add the brinjal and salt with the jaggery, and grind coarsely.

3. GINGER CHUTNEY

Ingredients

- 2" ginger, grated
- 1 tsp tamarind
- pinch of asafoetida
- 2 red chillies
- salt to taste
- ½ tsp mustard

Method

Fry the red chillies. Grind together all the ingredients except mustard. Season it with mustard.

4. COCONUT CHUTNEY

Ingredients

- ½ coconut, grated
- 5 green chillies
- 2 tbsps roasted gram
- ½ tsp black gram
- 1 bunch coriander leaves
- salt to taste
- ½ tsp mustard
- 1 curry leaf

Method

Grind together all the ingredients, except mustard, black gram and curry leaf, to a fine paste. Season with the remaining ingredients.

5. TOMATO CHUTNEY

Ingredients

- 2 ripe tomatoes, sliced
- salt to taste
- 1 clove garlic
- 2 tsps oil
- 1 tsp sugar
- 2 red chillies
- ½" ginger

Method

Grind together the chillies, garlic and ginger. Heat the oil and sauté the tomatoes with salt. When they are cooked, add the ground paste and sugar. Sauté for half a minute and remove from the fire.

6. MANGO CHUTNEY

Ingredients

- 6 large mangoes (half ripe)
- chilli powder to taste
- 1 tsp asafoetida
- 1 tbsp jaggery
- 1 cup oil
- salt to taste
- 1 tsp fenugreek
- ½ tsp turmeric
- 2 tsps mustard

Method

Grate the mangoes. Dry roast and powder the fenugreek. Heat the oil a pan. Splutter the mustard and add the other ingredients except chilli powder. When the mixture leaves the sides of the pan, add the fenugreek, asafoetida, chilli powder. Stir for a minute. Cool and grind to a fine paste.

7. KASHMIRI CHUTNEY

Ingredients

- 2 raw mangoes, chopped
- 1 tbsp sultanas
- 2 tbps chilli powder
- 2 tsps grated ginger
- salt to taste
- 2 tbsps vinegar
- 2 tomatoes, chopped
- 8 green chillies chopped
- 25 almonds, chopped
- 2 tbsps sugar
- 1 tsp mustard powder

Method

Mix together all the ingredients well. Bottle it immediately and keep it marinated in the fridge for a week before using it.

8. APPLE CHUTNEY

Ingredients

- 2 apples
- 1 tsp cardamom-clove powder
- 1 tsp cardamom-clove powder
- ½ tsp lemon juice
- ½ cup sugar
- 2 tbsps pepper powder
- ½ tsp cumin powder
- ½ tsp grated ginger
- salt to taste

Method

Cut the apples into small pieces. Heat water in a pan. Tie the apples in a cloth and dip in hot water till the pieces become soft. Remove the pieces form the cloth and cool. Crush into pulp with the addition of water. Add the sugar and ginger to the apple pulp, and heat the mixture till thick (when dropped form the spoon, it should fall in a sheet form). Remove from the fire. Add the spices, lemon juice and vinegar. Stir well.

9. GREEN CHUTNEY

Ingredients

- 1 bunch coriander leaves
- 1½ tbsps roasted gram
- 1 clove garlic
- salt to taste
- ¼ bunch mint leaves
- 15 green chillies
- 1" ginger
- ½ tsp pomegranate seeds

Method

Grind together all the ingredients into a smooth paste.

10. SWEET CHUTNEY

Ingredients

- 1 cup jaggery
- a handful of raisins
- ½ tsp cumin powder
- ¾ cup tamarind pulp
- 1½ tsps chilli powder
- ½ tsp rock salt

Method

Boil the jaggery and tamarind on low heat till the mixture turns shiny. Add all the other ingredients and bring to a boil. Remove from the fire and cool.

11. GRAPE SAUCE

Ingredients

- 1 tsp arrowroot powder
- 1 cup water
- ½ cup sugar
- 4 tbsps concentrated black grape juice
- 1 tsp lemon juice

Method

Blend the arrowroot with a little water. Add the grape juice, water, lemon juice and sugar. Heat it in a pan and bring it to a boil. Lower the heat and cool till the sauce becomes thick. Stir well so that no lump forms. Use this sauce for fruit salad topping or to decorate an ice-cream.

12. CUSTARD SAUCE

Ingredients

- 1 cup milk
- 2 tbsps sugar
- 1 tbsp custard powder

Method

Mix the custard with a little cold milk to a smooth paste. Heat the rest of the milk and sugar. When it starts boiling, add the paste, and cook till the sauce is thick. Remove from the fire and stir for a minute. Cool.

13. BRANDY BUTTER SAUCE

Ingredients

- 100 gms butter
- 2 tbsps brandy
- 100 gms icing sugar

Method

Cream the butter till fluffy. Add the icing sugar and continue to heat. Gradually add the brandy, blending well. Chill.

14. CARAMEL SAUCE

Ingredients

1 cup sugar
3 tbsps cream
5 tbsps water
1 tsp chopped nuts

Method

Heat the sugar with the till the mixture becomes golden brown. Cool and add the cream and nuts. Blend well.

15. CHOCOLATE-PEPPERMINT SAUCE

Ingredients

100 gms sugar
1 slab plain chocolate
½ cup condensed milk
20 gms butter
1 tsp peppermint essence

Method

Mix all the ingredients, except the essence, and heat in pan for about 10 minutes till thick. Add the essence and remove from heat. Cool and chill.

16. WHITE SAUCE

Ingredients

1 tbsp butter
1 cup milk
¼ cup flour
salt and pepper to taste

Method

Melt the fat, add the flour and stir until smooth. Cook over gentle heat for 2-3 minutes, stirring to avoid lumps forming. Bring to a boil, and continue to stir till the sauce thickens. Ad the salt and pepper, blend well and cool.

17. LEMON SAUCE

Ingredients

rind and juice of 1 lemon
1 tsp sugar
pepper to taste
1 cup white sauce
a dash of salt

Method

Add 2 tbsps water to the white sauce and heat it. Simmer the lemon rind in it for five minutes. Strain and boil the liquid till thick. Remove from the fire. Add the lemon juice, sugar, salt and pepper. Stir till the sugar dissolves and the ingredients have blended well.

18. CHEESE SAUCE

Ingredients

1 cup white sauce
a pinch of mustard powder
2 tbsps grated cheese
pepper and salt to taste

Method

Boil the sauce with a little water. Stir in the cheese and the seasoning. Cook till thick. Cool.

19. STRAW SAUCE

Ingredients

½ tin strawberries (or 1 cup fresh ones)
2 tbsps icing sugar
2 tbsps lemon juice

Method

Puree the strawberries. Add the icing sugar and lemon juice, and blend well. Chill this sauce.

20. HONEY SAUCE

Ingredients

½ cup figs + walnuts, chopped
½ cup honey
½ cup water

Method

Mix the honey and water, and heat well. Add the figs and walnuts. Chill till serving time.

21. POTATO RAITA

Ingredients

2 potatoes, boiled and finely chopped
1 cup curd
1 tbsp chopped coriander leaves
a dash of asafoetida
2 green chilles, chopped
salt to taste
½ tsp oil
¼ tsp mustard

Method

Mix all the ingredients with the potatoes and season with mustard and asafoetida.

22. CUCUMBER RAITA

Ingredients

2 cucumbers, grated with skin
1 tsp oil
1 cup curd
½ tsp mustard
2 green chillies, chopped
½ bunch coriander, chopped
1 tsp salt

Method

Squeeze out the water from the cucumber. Add the curd, salt, and the coriander leaves. Season with mustard and green chillies. Mix well.

BREAKFAST FARE

BREAKFAST FARE

1. DOSAS

Ingredients

3 cups rice (soaked for 2 hours)
2 tsps salt
2 tbsps fenugreek (soaked for 2 hours)
1 cup black gram (soaked 2 hours)
oil or ghee

Method

Grind the rice and dal with fenugreek separately. Mix the batter, add the salt and let it ferment overnight. The next day, heat a tawa (non-stuck). Smear a little ghee or oil, spread a ladle of batter on the tawa. When golden, turn the dosa and allow the other side also to turn golden. Serve hot with chutney and sambhar.

2. MYSORE MASALA DOSA

Ingredients

1 cup rice (soaked for 2 hours)
1 tbsp black gram (soaked for 2 hours)
¼ cup beaten rice (soaked for 1 hours)
½ tsp fenugreek

1 tbsp red gram (soaked for 2 hours)
1 tsp salt
(soaked for 2 hours)
1½ tbsps fine semolina
ghee or oil

Method

Grind together the rice, dals and beaten rice with fenugreek to a smooth consistency. Add the salt and allow to ferment overnight. Next day, mix the semolina. Heat a non-stick pan, smear with ghee or oil, and prepare the dosas. Place the potatoes filling in the centre, dot with butter and fold over into a semicircle, or shape into a triangle.

Stuffing

Cook 4 potatoes, peel and chop, and lightly mash. Cut the onion and 2 green chillies. Heat oil in a pan, splutter 1 tsp mustard, add the chopped onion, chillies and 1 tsp grated ginger, and 3-4 curry leaves. Add ½ tsp turmeric powder. When the onion turns pink, add the potatoes and salt according to taste. Remove from the fire and add 1 tbsp chopped coriander leaves. Mix well.

3. RAVA DOSA

Ingredients

1 cup semolina
½ cup rice flour
2 bunch coriander leaves, chopped
1 tsp cumin
1 cup maida
2 small onions, minced
4 green chillies, minced
salt to taste
oil of ghee

Method

Mix together all the ingredients with enough water to form a thin consistency batter. Heat a non-stick tawa, grease it with ghee or oil, and pour a ladleful of the batter on it. Do not use the ladle to spread but tilt the tawa on all sides so that the batter spreads on its own. When golden brown, flip and cook the other side. Serve hot with coconut chutney.

4. PESARATTU

Ingredients

- 1 cup whole green gram (soaked for 2 hours)
- 1 tsp grated ginger
- salt to taste
- 2 onions, minced
- 5 green chillies, chopped

Method

Grind the dal coarsely, using a little water. Add all the ingredients. Heat a non-stick tawa, and fry the pesarattus (or dosas) till crisp. Turn over and roast the other side too. Serve hot with chutney.

5. UTHAPPAM

Ingredients

- 2 cups raw rice (soaked for 3 hours)
- ¼ cup red gram (soaked for 3 hours)
- salt to taste
- oil
- 2 cups boiled rice (soaked for 3 hours)
- ½ cup black gram
- 1 tsp fenugreek (soaked for 3 hours)

Method

Grind together all the ingredients till smooth. Allow to ferment. Heat a non-stick tawa and spread a ladle of the butter on it. Fry on both sides. Serve hot with chutney.

Variations

You can add onions, tomatoes, paneer, capsicum, carrot on top of the uthappam while it is being cooled. When you add these, use oil on both sides to cook the vegetables.

6. UPPUMA

Ingredients

- 2 cups semolina
- 3 onions, chopped
- 1" ginger, grated
- 1 tsp Bengal gram
- 2 tbsps oil
- 4½ cups water
- salt to taste
- 6 curry leaves
- 1 tsp mustard
- 2 tsps ghee

Method

Dry roast the semolina till golden. Heat the oil in a pan. Splutter the mustard, and add the dals. When they turn brown, add the curry leaves, onions, chillies and ginger. Sauté till the onions turn pink. Add the water and salt. When the water starts boiling, add the semolina, lower the heat, stir well and close the vessel with a lid. After a minute, stir the uppuma well. Add the ghee and cook for 2 minutes more. Serve hot.

Variations

You can add cooked peas, carrots, capsicums, potatoes, beans.

7. VERMICELLI UPPUMA

Ingredients

- 2 cups vermicelli
- 4 green chillies, chopped
- 2 tsps ghee
- ½ cup shredded cabbage
- 1 potato, boiled and chopped
- 4 tbsps oil
- 2 tomatoes, chopped
- 1 tsp Bengal gram
- 6 curry leaves
- 2 onions, chopped
- ½ tsp turmeric powder
- 1 large carrot, chopped
- 1 capsicum, chopped
- 2 tbsps peas, cooked
- salt to taste
- juice of 1 lemon
- ¼ tsp mustard
- 1 tbsp cashews, sliced

Method

Heat the ghee and fry the vermicelli till golden brown. Heat 6 cups of water with a tsp of oil and a little salt. When it boils, add the vermicelli and cook till tender. Drain in a colander, and pour cold water on top to prevent them sticking. Heat the oil and add the mustard, Bengal gam, curry leaves and cashews. When the mustard splutters, add the onions, chillies and vegetables. Fry on medium heat till they become soft. Add the vermicelli, salt and turmeric, and sauté for about 2 minutes. Squeeze the lemon juice over it and mix well.

8. BREAD UPPUMA

Ingredients

- 4 slices bread, cut into fine pieces
- ½ tsp grated ginger
- ½ tsp mustard
- salt to taste
- 1 onion, chopped
- 1 green chilli, chopped
- 3 curry leaves
- 1 tsp Bengal gram

Method

Heat the oil in a pan. Splutter the mustard and add the Bengal gram. When it becomes red, add the onions, chillies, curry leaves and ginger and sauté for two or three minutes till the onion becomes translucent. Add the bread pieces and salt and stir well. On low heat sauté the bread pieces, add the ghee little by little until the bread pieces become brown and crisp. Serve hot.

9. IDLI

Ingredients

- 3 cups parboiled rice
- 1 tsp fenugreek
- 1 cup black gram
- salt to taste

Method

Soak the rice and dal with fenugreek separately for three hours. Grind the rice to semolina consistency, and the dal to a fine and smooth texture. Combine and mix well. Add the salt and stir. Let it ferment. Heat water in a pressure cooler. Fill the idli moulds with the batter and steam the idlis for 7-8 minutes. Remove and serve hot with coconut chutney and sambhar.

Variations

You can add onions, or carrots and peas, coriander and curry leaves, or season with mustard and Bengal gram.

10. RAVA IDLI

Ingredients

- 2 cups semolina, roasted dry
- 2 cups sour curd
- salt to taste
- ½ tsp mustard
- ½ Bengal gram
- 1 tsp black gram
- 5 tbsps oil
- 4 green chillies, minced
- 2 tbsps curry-coriander leaves
- ½ tsp cooking soda
- 1½ tbsps cashew, broken

Method

Mix together the semolina and curd. Heat the oil and add the mustard, dals and cashews. When the mustard splutters pour over the semolina. Add the salt, chillies, leaves and soda. Mix well and steam the idlis in greased idli moulds for 7-8 minutes. Remove and serve hot with coconut chutney and sambhar.

RICE PREPARATIONS

RICE PREPARATIONS

1. PEAS-CORN BIRIYANI

Ingredients

- 2 cups basmati rice
- 250 gms peas, boiled
- oil for frying
- 2 black cardamoms
- 8 peppercorns
- 2 bay leaves
- 2 tsps coriander powder
- 2 tsps ginger-garlic paste
- ½ tsp turmeric powder
- 6 tomatoes, chopped
- 2 tbsps chopped ginger
- 1 tbsps chopped coriander leaves
- 2 tsp salt
- 250 gms corn
- 5 green cardamoms
- 8 cloves
- 1 stick cinnamon
- 2 tsps chilli powder
- 2 medium onions, chopped
- 2 green chillies, deseeded and chopped
- 1 cup thick curds
- salt to taste

For the Assembling

- A pinch of saffron, soaked in ½ cup milk
- 2 tsps garam masala powder
- 50 gms butter, cubed
- ½ cup chopped mint leaves

Method

Boil the rice with salt and set aside. Pressure cook the corn till soft. Put 2 tbsps oil in a pan. Add the cardamoms, cloves, peppercorms, cinnamon, bay leaves and the chilli-coriander powders. Sauté for a minute. Add the copped onions and fry till pink. Add the ginger-garlic paste and sauté for another two minutes. Add the chillies, turmeric powder, curds and tomatoes. Cook till the masala leaves the oil. Add the peas and corn, chopped ginger, coriander leaves and a little water. Simmer it for a few minutes till the gravy is thick. To assemble, arrange half the peas-corn in a greased baking dish. Put a layer of rice on top of this. Then drizzle a little saffron milk on this, and sprinkle some garma masala powder. Place a few mint leaves and a few cubes of butter. Repeat this on the second layer too. Seal the dish with a foil and bake for about half an hour in a preheated oven. Serve hot.

2. HARA BHARA PULAO

Ingredients

- 1 cup basmati rice
- 2 cinnamon sticks
- 7 peppercorns
- 2 cardamoms
- 2 green chillies, chopped
- 2 tsps coriander leaves
- ½ tsp garam masala powder
- chilli-ginger paste
- 250 gms cauliflower, cut into small florets
- 4 cloves
- 2 bay leaves
- 2 onions, chopped
- 4 tbsps oil
- salt to taste

Method

Heat 1 tbsp oil in a pan. Fry the bay leaves, cloves, cinnamon, peppercorns for half a minute on medium heat. Add the onions, green chillies and saute till pink. Keep aside. Heat the remaining oil and fry the vegetables for five minutes. Add the paste, the fried onions, garam masala and salt. Stir-fry for five minutes. Add the washed rice, and 2 cups and a little more water. Cool on medium heat. Stir rice once while cooking. When done, garnish with coriander.

3. JEERA RICE

Ingredients

- 2 cups basmati rice
- 1 tsp cuminseeds
- 2 tbsps oil
- 1 onion, chopped
- 2 tsps cumin powder
- salt to taste

Method

Add nearly four cups of water in a pan and soak the rice. In another pan, heat the oil and splutter the cuminseeds. Add the onion and sauté till transparent. Add the cumin powder and stir, add the rice and salt and mix well. Pressure cook till done. Serve hot.

4. VEGETABLE BIRYANI

Ingredients

- 2 cups basmati rice
- 150 gms peas
- salt to taste
- 1" cinnamon
- 4 cloves
- 4 tomatoes, chopped
- 4 tbsps oil
- 3 tbsps dry fruits
- 1 cup mixed vegetables, chopped
- 2 green chillies, chopped
- 1 tsp chilli powder
- 2 tsps caraway seeds
- ½ tsp pepper powder
- ½ cup curd
- ½ tsp mustard

Method

Cook the rice with salt, 3¾ cups water and 2 tbsps dry fruits in a pressure cooker cooker. Fry the vegetables and the peas. Keep aside. In the same pan, splutter the mustard. Add the green chillies, cinnamon, caraway, cloves, and pepper powder. Sauté for half a minute, and then add the onions. Fry till the onions become pink. Add the salt and chilli powder, and stir. Add the tomatoes and fry till cooked. Add the vegetables, stir well, then add the cooked rice. Mix well but gently so that the rice grains do not break. Cook on low fire for three more minutes. Garnish with dry fruits and coriander leaves.

5. KHICHDI

Ingredients

- 1 cup rice
- ½ cup ghee
- 1" cinnamon
- 4 peppercorns
- 1 cup split green gram
- 2 bay leaves
- 4 cloves
- salt to taste

Method

Heat the ghee in a pressure pan. Add the whole spices. Sauté for a few seconds. Add the rice and dal. Sauté till the mixture is pink and aromatic. Add 4 cups of boiling water and salt, and cook on a very low flame till the khichdi is done. Serve hot.

6. CHANA DAL PULAO

Ingredients

- 1½ cups basmati rice
- ½ tsp cumin
- 2" cinnamon
- 2 bay leaves
- 2¾ cups water
- salt to taste
- ¾ cup bengal gram (soaked for 2 hours)
- 4 cloves
- 2 black cardamoms
- 2 tbsps oil

Method

Heat the oil in a pressure pan. Add the cumin, cloves, cardamoms, bay leaves and fry for three minutes. Add the rice and dal and sauté for a minute. Add the salt and water and pressure cook until rice and dal are cooked. Serve hot.

7. PEAS PULAO

Ingredients

2 cups basmati rice
2 black cardamoms
2" cinnamon
2 bay leaves
salt to taste

1 cup shelled peas
10 peppercorns
5 cloves
2 tbsps oil
3 cups water

Method

Heat the oil in a pressure pan. Add all the spices and sauté for a minute. Add the peas and stir-fry for a minute. Now add the rice and fry for another minute. Add the water and salt, and pressure cook till the rice is cooked and grainy. Serve hot.

8. BAKALA BHATH

Ingredients

6 cups cooked rice
2 cups curds
1 cucumber, grated with the skin
1 tsp Bengal gram
a dash of asafoetida
1 stalk curry leaves
1 green chilli, chopped
1 tbsp grated ginger

1 cup warm milk
1 carrot, grated
½ cup grated coconut
½ tsp mustard
1 tsp cumin
2 tbsps peanuts
1 pinch coriander, chopped
salt to taste

Method

Mix the milk with the rice well. Add the curds and mix again. Add the carrot and cucumber a well as the coconut. Mix well mustard, bengal gram, asafoetida, cumin, peanuts, ginger, green chilli and curry leaves. Garnish with the coriander leaves.

9. VANGIBHATH

Ingredients

- 1 kg brinjals, halved and cut into finger lengths
- a pinch of asafoetida
- 1 tsp bengal gram
- 1 tsp fennel
- 2 tbsps peanuts
- 1 stalk curry leaves
- ½ tbsp grated coconut
- 2 tsps vangibhath powder
- 1 capsicum, chopped
- ½ tsp mustard
- 1 tsp cumin
- 2 tbsps sesame
- 3 tbsps grated ginger
- 1 bunch coriander, chopped
- salt to taste
- juice of 1 lemon

Method

Heat the oil, and fry the asafoetida, mustard, cumin, fennel and bengal gram. When the seeds splutter, add the sesame and peanuts. Add the ginger, coriander and curry leaves and turmeric. Cook and stir for a little while. Add the brinjals and capsicums and stir-fry for a minute. Sprinkle a little water, cover and cook till the brinjals are done and soft. Then add the coconut, salt and vangibhath powder. Add the cooked rice and mix well, then add the juice to taste. Serve hot.

10. MANGO RICE

Ingredients

- 6 cups cooked rice
- 1 cup grated coconut
- a dash of asafoetida
- 4 green raw mangoes
- 1 tsp turmeric powder
- salt to taste

Frying Ingredients

- a dash of asafoetida
- 1 tsp fenugreek
- 1 tbsp bengal gram
- 2-3 tbsps peanuts
- ½ tsp mustard
- 1 tsp cumin
- 1 tbsp black gram
- 2 green chillies, chopped

1 bunch coriander, chopped
1" ginger, grated
1 stalk curry leaves
1 tbsp oil

Method

To make a paste of the mango, peel the skin and chop the mangoes into pieces. Heat the oil, add the mustard and bengal gram. Cook until the dal turns brown and the mustard splutters. Add the leaves, ginger and chillies. Mix well and cook for a while. Add the ground paste and salt to taste. Cook till the mixture is firm. Remove from the heat. Add to the cooked rice, mix well. Serve hot.

11. LEMON RICE

Ingredients

6 cups cooked rice
2 tbsps oil
1 tsp ajwain
1 tsp bengal gram
2 tbsps peanuts
1 bunch coriander leaves, chopped
1 tsp grated ginger
juice of 2 large lemons
2 dash of asafoetida
1 tsp mustard
1 tsp fenugreek
1 tsp cumin
1 red chilli, halved
1 stalk curry leaves
½ tsp turmeric powder
½ cup grated coconut
salt to taste

Method

Heat the oil in a pan. Add the dry ingredients. When the mustard splutters, add the leaves, rice, salt and coconut. Remove from the heat and add the lemon juice. Stir well and serve hot.

12. PUDINA PULAO

Ingredients

2 cups basmati rice
1 cup peas
3 potatoes, chopped
1 bunch mint, chopped

8 green chillies, chopped
1 tsp grated ginger
½ tsp turmeric
4 cloves
1 bay leaf
2 tbsps oil
½ coconut, grated
3 onions, chopped
½ lemon
2 cardamoms
salt to taste

Method

Cook the rice with salt. Grind together the coconut, mint, chillies, turmeric and ginger. Boil the potatoes and peas with salt. Fry the onions in hot oil. Saute till they turn pink. Add the vegetables and saute for a minute. Add the ground masala and saute for five minutes. Add the rice and stir on slow fire till well mixed. Remove from the fire, add the lemon juice and stir well. Serve hot.

13. TAMARIND RICE

Ingredients

2 cups cooked rice
2 tbsps jaggery
2 tbsps rasam powder
1 tbsps bengal gram
a pinch of asafoetida
3 tbsps peanuts
curry leaves
6-8 red chillies
1 large lemon-size tamarind ball
salt to taste
1 tsp mustard
1 tbsps black gram
3 tbsps dried gram (horsegram)
2 tbsps gingelly oil

Dry-fry and Powder

¼ cup sesame
3 tsps pepper
1 copra
2 tsps fenugreek
2 tsps cumin

Method

Extract the pulp from the tamarind. Heat the oil and add the mustard, dals, asafoetida, peanuts, chillies and curry leaves. When the mustard splutters, add the tamarind extract, jaggery, salt and rasam powder. Cook till the mixture becomes concentrated. Remove from the fire. Add the cooked rice and salt. Mix well. Add the dry powder and mix well again. Serve hot.

CHAPATIS AND PARATHAS

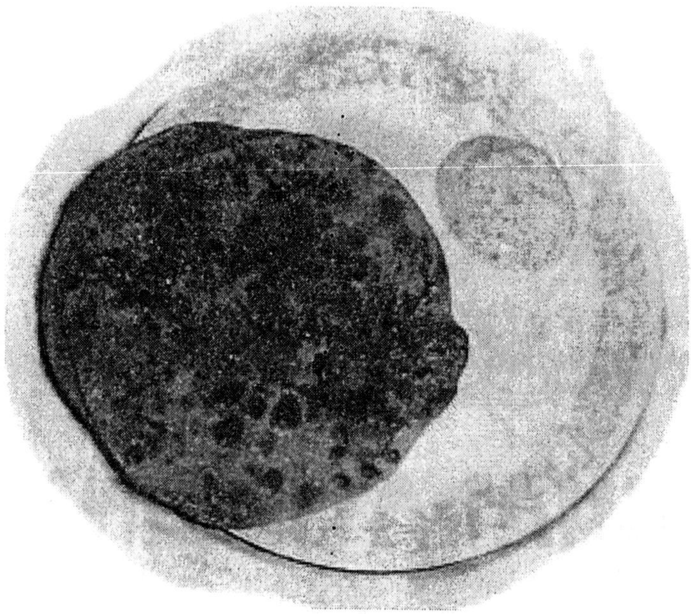

CHAPATIS AND PARATHAS

1. ALOO KA PARATHA

Ingredients

2 cups wheat four

1 tsp salt

For the Filling

4 potatoes, boil and mashed

1 small onion, finely chopped

1 tsp chilli powder

salt to taste

¼ tsp turmeric powder

3 green chillies, finely chopped

1 tbsp dry fenugreek leaves

ghee or vegetable oil

Method

Knead the flour with salt and water to form a pliable dough. Add the fenugreek leaves, chillies and onion to the mashed potatoes. Also add the turmeric and chilli powders as well as salt. Mix well. Roll out each lemon-sized ball of dough. Place a tablespoon of the potato filling in the centre, close it from all sides. Roll out again very carefully and cook on the tawa, applying the ghee on both sides until light brown and crisp. Serve hot with chutney or pickle or plain curd.

2. GOBHI KA PARATHA

Ingredients

2 cups wheat flour
salt to taste

Fir the Filling

2 cups grated cauliflower
1 tsp chilli powder
salt to taste
ghee for the parathas
3 green chillies
chopped coriander
½ tsp garam masala powder

Method

Knead the flour and salt with enough water to make a smooth dough. Add all the ingredients to the cauliflower and mix well. Divide the dough into equal portions. Roll out the chapatis, place the cauliflower filling in the centre of each, close form all sides, and carefully roll out the parathas. Fry each one on the tawa, applying ghee on both sides till light brown and crisp.

Variations

You can use cooked dal; cooked peas (mashed); grated radish in place of cauliflower. You can also use carrots.

3. NAAN

Ingredients

3 cups maida
½ cup curd
1 tbsp oil
¼ tsp sugar
¼ cup ajwain or sesame
½ cup baking powder
½ cup milk
2 tbsps butter
salt to taste

Method

Sieve the maida with the baking powder. Add the salt, sugar, curd, oil and butter, and mix well with fingers. Add the milk and water (if required) a little at a time to form a very smooth dough. Cover with a wet cloth and set aside for at least two hours. Divide into medium size balls of equal portions. Roll the ball in sesame seeds, apply some flour and roll out into a thick round. Place it in a preheated tandoor or even (350°F) on a greased tray. Bake till golden brown on both sides. Serve hot, topped with butter.

4. BHATURA

Ingredients

1 cup maida
½ tsp baking powder
salt to taste
1 cup curd
oil for frying

Method

Sieve the flour with baking powder. Add the curd and salt, and mix well. Knead into a medium soft dough, using water if necessary. Set aside in a warm place for at least two hours. Knead once again before dividing into equal size balls. Roll out the bhaturas and deep fry till golden. Serve hot with chana masala.

5. TANDOORI ROTI

Ingredients

2 cups wheat flour
2 tsps baking powder
½ cup milk
salt to taste
½ cup maida
½ cup curd
2 tbsps ghee

Method

Sieve the flours and baking powder. Add the salt, curd and milk little by little until a soft dough is got. Set aside for at least half an hour. Knead the dough again for half a minute. Divide the dough into equal portions. Roll out into thick oblong/circular rotis. Apply ghee on both sides and bake in a tandoor or oven till the rotis are crisp and cooked.

6. BESAN ATTA ROTI

Ingredients

2 cups wheat flour
1 bunch coriander, finely chopped
2 tbsps grated coconut
ghee
1 cup besan flour
juice of ½ lemon
a pinch of sugar
½ tsp chilli powder

Method

Prepare the dough using the flours with salt and water to form a soft dough. Mix together the other ingredients for the filling. Divide the dough into equal portions. Form balls, and press down the centre of each. Stuff with the filling, close and roll out. Deep fry and serve hot.

7. DAL PHULKA

Ingredients

125 gms green gram (soaked for 15 minutes)
30 gms ghee
¼ tsp turmeric powder
2 tbsps chopped coriander leaves
150 gms flour
1 tsp chilli powder
salt to taste
1 small onion, finely chopped

Method

Cook the dal with salt and turmeric till soft. Mix the onions, chillies and leaves with the dal. Add the chilli powder and mix well. Rub the ghee in the flour and add enough water to make a stiff dough. Divide into equal portions. Form into balls, press down the centre, stuff with the dal mixture, cover and roll out. Fry till brown and crisp, using ghee on both sides.

8. METHI ROTI

Ingredients

100 gms flour
50 gms fenugreek leaves, finely chopped
salt to taste
2 tbsps ghee
50 gms besan flour
1 bunch coriander, chopped
¼ tsp turmeric powder

Method

Add the salt and ghee to the flours and form into a smooth dough with water. Add the leaves and knead again. Divide into equal portions. Roll out each ball. Apply ghee and roll up again into a ball. Roll out and fry on a tawa with ghee.

9. MAIZE ROTI

Ingredients

375 gms maize flour
2 tbsps finely chopped fenugreek leaves
salt to taste
1 tbsp ghee

Method

Mix the ghee in the flour with fingers. Add the salt, leaves and water to make a smooth dough. Divide into 6-8 balls. Roll out thin and fry on a tawa without oil.

10. PANEER-MATAR PARATHA

Ingredients

100 gms wheat flour
2 cups milk
1 green chilli, chopped
2 tbsps ghee
coriander leaves
100 gms peas, cooked and mashed
½ tbsp lemon jucie
1 tbsp chopped

Method

Knead the flour with water into a smooth dough. Heat the milk and curdle it with the lemon juice. Strain and keep the chenna (paneer). In 1 tbsp ghee, fry the peas. Remove. Add the chillies, paneer and salt, and mix well. Divide the dough into small balls. Roll out each, place the filling in the centre, close and roll out again. Fry the parathas on a tawa, applying ghee on both sides. Serve hot.

11. MISSI ROTI

Ingredients

200 gms maida
200 gms spinach, chopped finely
salt to taste
200gms besan
200gms onion, chopped finely

Method

Sift together the flours and salt. Knead this into a smooth, stiff dough, using just enough water to make the dough pliable. Divide the dough into small balls. Roll out each chapati. Mix the spinach, onion and salt. Place a tbsp of this mixture in half of the rotis. Use the remaining rotis to cover the spinach sealing the edges of both rotis. Gently roll out the chapatis. Cook on a medium flame on a hot tawa till light brown. Turn over the roti and cook the other side. Remove from the tawa and spread a dash of ghee on it. Serve hot.

VEGETABLE BONANZA

VEGETABLE BONANZA

1. KASHMIRI MALAI BAINGAN

Ingredients

- ½ kg brinjals (long ones)
- salt to taste
- 20 gms cuminseeds, powdered coarsely
- ½ tsp chilli powder
- 1 tsp turmeric powder
- oil for deep frying
- 1 tsp sugar
- ½ tsp tomato puree
- 2 cups cream

Method

Wash the brinjals, and cut them into medium-sized pieces. Sprinkle with salt and turmeric powder, and set aside for 2 minutes. Heat the oil in a pan, and fry the marinated brinjal pieces till golden. Remove and set aside. In the same oil, fry the coarsely ground cumin till brown. Add the sugar and chilli powder. Mix well and add the tomato puree. Keep stirring till the paste turns light brown. Remove from heat and allow to cool. Stir in the cream gradually. When fully mixed, add the fried brinjal pieces, one by one, till all the pieces are steeped well in the paste. Over low heat, warm the brinjals. Serve hot with rice or roti.

2. SPINACH-CORN COMBINE

Ingredients

- 4 tender corncobs
- 1 small bunch coriander. finely chopped
- 1 tbsp khus-khus
- 4 tsps ghee or oil
- 2 onions, finely chopped
- salt to taste
- ½ tbsp chilli powder
- ½ cup water
- 2-3 bunches of spinach, chopped
- 3 tbsps grated coconut
- 2 green chillies, chopped
- 1 tsp cuminseeds
- 8-10 cashewnuts
- a pinch of sugar

Method

Boil the corncobs in water for 2-3 minutes. Remove from heat, cool and separate the corn kernels from the cobs. Set aside. Pressure cook the spinach. Remove and cool. In a mixer, blend the spinach with the coriander leaves to a fine paste. Set aside. Grind the coconut, khus-khus and green chillies together to make a paste. Set aside. Heat the oil in a pan. Add the cuminseeds. When they crackle, add the cashewnuts and chopped onions. Fry till golden. Remove from the pan and set aside in a separate bowl. In the remaining oil, fry the spinach paste. Remove. Fry the coconut mix till light brown. Add the salt, sugar, chilli, powder, corn kernels, spinach paste and the fried onions. Add the water and mix well. Bring to a boil. Remove, garnish with cream if required, and serve hot with rice or rotis.

3. SCRAMBLED CHEESE

Ingredients

- 1 lt milk (skimmed)
- 2 tbsps oil
- 1 green chilli, finely chopped
- 1 tbsp chilli vinegar
- 1 onion, finely chopped
- salt to taste

½ tsp chilli powder
3 tbsps chopped spring onions
½ tsp coriander powder
1 carrot, grated
½ tsp roasted cumin powder
½ tsp garam masala powder

Method

Heat the skimmed milk and add the vinegar, once it starts boiling. When the milk curdles, pass it through a mesh to obtain paneer (cheese). Wash with water strain to remove the moisture and crush it coarsely. Set aside. Heat the oil in a pan. Add the grated carrot, chopped spring onions and stir continuously. Add the paneer and mix thoroughly over low heat. Add the powders and stir well. Serve hot with rice or roti.

4. TOMATO-PANEER CHAMAN

Ingredients

100 gms tomatoes
1 tsp garam masala powder
1 tsp chilli powder
2 tbsps cashewnut paste
40 gms cream
50 gms butter
2 tsps ginger-garlic paste
salt to taste
1 tsp kasoori methi powder
300 gms paneer

Method

Boil the tomatoes in water. Cool and drain. Reserve the water. Puree the tomatoes and set aside. Heat 2 tsps of oil in a pan. Add the puree, garlic-ginger paste, garam masala and tomato water. Cook for 5 minutes. Add the salt, chilli and kasoori methi powders, cashewnut paste, butter and cream. Keep stirring over medium heat till the mixture thickens. Add the paneer cubes, and cook for 5-9 minutes. Serve hot with roti or rice.

5. BHINDI MASALA

Ingredients

- 2 cups lady'sfinger, cut into 1" pieces
- ¼ tsp turmeric powder
- ½ tsp dry mango powder
- ½ tsp garam masala
- ½ tsp ajwain
- ½ cup gram flour (besan)
- 1 tsp coriander powder
- 1 tsp fennel powder
- 1 tbsp oil
- salt to taste
- ½ tsp chilli powder

Method

Lightly dry-fry the besan in a pan on low flame till a fine smell emanates. Add the coriander, chilli, fennel and garam masala powder and blend well. Heat oil in a pan and add the ajwain in it, then the lady'sfinger and salt, turmeric and mango powders. Stir and cook covered till the vegetable is done. Add the besan mixture. Stir well and saute till the vegetable is well coated. Serve hot, with rice or roti. You can garnish it with coriander leaves or 3-4 mint leaves.

6. POTATO-BHINDI COMBINE

Ingredients

- 50 gms lady'sfinger (bhindi) cut into ½" pieces
- 2 tbsps oil
- 1 tsp coriander powder
- ½ tsp cumin
- 1 tsp dry mango powder
- 50 gms potato, boiled, peeled and cubes
- ½ tsp turmeric powder
- 1 tsp chilli powder
- ½ tsp ajwain
- salt to taste

Method

Heat oil in a pan. Add the cumin and ajwain. Saute for a minute, then add the vegetables. Add the salt, turmeric and mango powders. Lower the flame and cook covered till the vegetables are done. Uncover, add the coriander and chilli powders. Mix well and saute till all the moisture evaporates. Serve hot with roti.

7. STUFFED LADY'SFINGERS

Ingredients

15-20 lady'sfingers, slit lengthwise
2 tsp coriander powder
1 tsp chilli powder
2 tsps fennel seeds powder
1 tsp ajwain
1 tsp green chillies, finely chopped
½ cup finely chopped onion
½ turmeric powder
1 tsp dry mango powder
2 tbsps oil
1 tsp grated ginger
salt to taste

Method

Mix all the ingredients except the bhindis, ajwain and oil. Stuff the bhindis with this mixture. Heat oil in a pan. Add the ajwain, saute for a few seconds, then add the stuffed bhindis. Cook covered till the bhindis are well cooked. Remove the cover and cook till the moisture evaporates. Serve hot with rotis or parathas.

8. CHATPATE BAINGAN

Ingredients

8-10small brinjals
1 tsp ginger paste
2 onions, finely chopped
3 tbsps tamarind pulp
½ tsp coriander powder
salt to taste
1 tbsp finely chopped coriander leaves
½ cup oil
8-10 curry leaves
3 tomatoes, finely chopped
½ tsp chilli powder
½ tsp cumin powder

Method

Make four slits along the length of the brinjals, taking care to keep the stem infact. Heat oil in a pan, and fry the brinjals for 3-4 minutes. Keep aside. Fry the onion until golden brown. Add the ginger paste and curry leaves, fry for 2-3 minutes, then add the tomatoes and fry for two minutes. Add the chilli, coriander and cumin powders, salt and tamarind pulp. Bring to a boil. Carefully add the brinjals. Add the coriander leaves and cook covered till the brinjals become tender. Serve hot with rice or chapatis.

9. KASHMIRI DUM ALOO

Ingredients

18-20 small-sized potatoes
5-6 dry kashmiri chillies
½ tsp cardamom powder
2 tbsps fennel powder
¼ tsp clove powder
salt to taste
½ tsp garam masala powder
oil to deep fry
2 cups curd
1 tsp dry ginger powder
¼ cup mustard oil
a pinch of asafoetida
½ tsp roasted cumin powder

Method

Peel and prick the potatoes all over with a fork. keep in salted water for 15 minutes. Heat oil in a pan, and fry the potatoes on medium flame till golden brown. Make a paste of red chillies. Whisk the curds with the paste, cardamom, ginger and fennel powders. Heat the mustard oil in a pan. Add the clove and asafoetida. Add the half a cup of water chilli paste, and salt, and bring to a boil. Stir in the curd mixture and boil. Add the fried potatoes, and cook till the potatoes absorb the gravy, and oil floats on top. Serve hot, garnished with cumin and garam masala powders.

10. PALAK PANEER

Ingredients

- ½ spinach, chopped
- 1 onion, chopped
- 2-3 bay leaves
- ¼ tsp pepper powder
- ½ tsp green chilli paste
- salt to taste
- 1 tsp garam masala
- 100 gms cottage cheese, cubed
- 3 tbsps butter
- 1 tsp cumin
- ¾ tps ginger garlic paste
- 2 tbsps vegetable oil

Method

Mix together the spinach, ginger-garlic paste, with some water. Pressure cook till just before the first whistle. Heat the oil in a pan. Fry the cheese on medium heat till they turn slightly brown. Set aside. Heat 2 tbsps of butter. Fry the bay leaves and cumin. Add the onions and fry till the onions turn pink. Add the salt, pepper and garam masala powder. Stir well. Add the cottage cheese and pureed spinach. Mix well. Put the mixture in a baking tray. Add the rest of the butter. Bake for half an hour at 180°C. Serve hot.

11. BAINGAN BHARTA

Ingredients

- 1 medium-sized brinjal (round)
- 1 tomato, finely chopped
- ½ tsp garam masala powder
- 3 tbsps vegetable oil
- salt to taste
- ½ cup peas, cooked
- 1 onion, finely chopped
- 1 green chilli, finely chopped
- ½ tsp chilli powder
- ¼ tsp turmeric powder
- chopped green coriander leaves for garnishing

Method

Brush the brinjal with oil and roast it on a gas burner over medium heat. Frequently turn it upside down, until fully roasted. Once done, hold it under cold running water or in a bowl of water. Cool and peel off the blackened skin. Mash the pulp. Heat oil in a pan. Add the green chilli and onion, and fry over medium heat until light golden brown. Add the chilli powder, turmeric powder, garam masala and salt, and stir. Add the tomatoes and cook until tender. Add the peas and mashed brinjal. Stir well. Fry for five minutes over medium hat. Garnish with green coriander leaves and serve hot.

12. HANDI KARELA

Ingredients

- 4 bittergourd
- 1 tsp chilli powder
- 1 tsp poppy seeds
- 1 tbsp gram flour, roasted lightly
- 1 tsp ginger
- 1 tbsp coriander leaves
- 1 tsp chopped coriander powder
- ¼ tsp garam masala
- 2 tbsps peanuts, crushed coarsely
- ½ tsp mustard
- 2 tsps salt
- ¼ turmeric powder
- ¼ cup coconut
- 4 pinches of asafoetida
- ½ tsp garlic, crushed
- 2 onions, finely chopped
- 1 tsp dried mango powder
- salt to taste
- ½ tsp cumin
- 1 tbsp jaggery
- 1 tomato, chopped
- 2 tbsps oil

Method

Wash and slit the gourds. Stuff with 2 tsps salt along the slits and sprinkle some on top too. Keep aside for an hour. Place under some heavy weight for 6 hours to allow the bitter water to drain out. When tender, remove the inside seeds, and rinse in tap water. Wipe dry with a kitchen towel. Rub with a few drops of white vinegar or lime. Mix the dry masalas, peanuts (half), coconut (half), poppy seeds and gram flour. Stuff the masala prepared into the gourds, keeping aside half for gravy. Heat oil in a heavy bottomed pan, put in the gourds, frying one at a time for half a minute. Drain, keep aside. Add the cumin and asafoetida, allow to splutter. Add the ginger, garlic and stir. Add the onions, fry till light pink. Add the tomato, remaining masala mixture coconut, peanuts, tomato and salt, and cook till the oil is released. Add the cream, stir-fry till the whiteness is reduced. Add the jaggery and stir till it dissolves. Add ¾ cup water, bring it to a bowl. Leave in the gourds, and gently arrange for even cooking. Cover, seal and allow to cook on low flame for 10-12 minutes. Before serving, break the seal, evaporate any leftover water on low fire. Increase sweetness by adding more jaggery if desired. Garnish with coriander, serve hot with parathas or steamed rice.

13. KADAI CAULIFLOWER

Ingredients

- 1 medium cauliflower, broken into florets
- 2 green chillies, slit
- ½ tsp cumin
- ¼ tsp turmeric powder
- 1 small capsicum, cut in slivers
- 1 tsp chopped coriander leaves
- 2 tbsps curds, beaten
- 1 onion, chopped finely
- ½ tsp grated ginger
- ½ tsp coriander powder
- 2 pinches asafoetida
- 1 tomato, chopped
- ½ tsp crushed garlic
- 1 tsp chilli powder
- 2 tbsps oil
- ½ tsp garam masala powder

Method

Boil the florets for 2-3 minutes. Drain and keep aside. Heat the oil in a pan, fry the chillies and remove from the oil. Add the cumin and allow it to splutter. Add the ginger, garlic and capsicum. Add the onions, tomatoes, stir-fry for two minutes. Add the masala paste, stir, cook till the oil separates. Add the cauliflower, stir gently, to mix well. When the oil separates, remove from the fire. Garnish with coriander leaves and fried chillies.

14. SHAHI PANEER

Ingredients

- 250 gms cottage cheese
- 2 green chillies, chopped fine
- ½ tsp chilli powder
- 3 tbsps butter
- 4 tomatoes, chopped fine
- ½ tsp garam masala powder
- 2 tbsps tomato sauce
- 1 onion, chopped into strips
- 2 cardamoms, crushed
- salt to taste
- ½ inch ginger, grated
- ½ cup beaten curd
- ½ cup milk

To Garnish

- 2 tbsps grated cheese
- 2 tbsp chopped coriander leaves

Method

Chop the cheese into 2-inch finger-sized pieces, heat half the butter. Add the onions, ginger, green chilli and cardamom. Fry for three to four minutes. Add the tomatoes, and cook for seven minutes, with the pan covered. Add the curd and cook for five minutes. Add half cup water and cool. Puree the mixture. Heat the remaining ghee, add the pureed gravy and all other ingredients except milk and cheese. Boil till the gravy becomes thick. Just before serving, heat the gravy, add the milk and cheese fingers, and boil for five minutes. Garnish with coriander leaves and grated cheese.

15. NAVRATTAN KURMA

Ingredients

- 2 cups peas, boiled
- 1 large carrot, chopped and boiled
- 2 tbsps fresh cottage cheese
- 1 small sweet lime (mosambi), cut into small pieces
- 2 cherries for decoration
- 2 slices pineapple, chopped
- 20 raisins
- ½ cup tomato sauce
- ¼ cup curd
- ¼ cup cream
- 3 tbsps butter
- 1 small apple, chopped
- 1 banana, chopped
- 10-15 cashewnuts
- 1 tbsp chopped coriander leaves
- 1 tbsps ghee

Dry Masalas

- 1 tsp cumin
- 2 tsps poppy seeds
- 1 tsp cardamom

Wet Masala

- 1 large onion
- 3 green chillies
- ¼ cup coconut shreds

Method

Grind the coconut, green chillies and cheese to a fine paste. Heat the butter, add the paste, the dry masalas, tomato puree, and stir-fry for two-three minutes. Add the peas, carrot, curds and stir-fry for five minutes. Add all the fruits, cream, cashews, raisins, and salt and remove from the fire. Mix thoroughly till the ingredients are well blended. Garnish with cherries and cheese before serving.

16. CHEESE-CORN-CAPSICUM

Ingredients

8-10 medium-sized capsicums
½ cup grated cheese
2-3 flakes garlic, ground to a paste
salt to taste
¾ cup corn kernels, boiled
1 inch piece ginger, ground to a paste
1 tbsp oil
1 tsp sugar

Method

Heat the oil in a pan. Add the ground pastes and fry for a minute. Add the corn, cheese, sugar and salt. Stir well, and cook till the gravy is thick. Slit the capsicums horizontally just below the stalk. Scoop out the seeds. Place the capsicums in boiling water and simmer for two-three minutes. Drain and place on kitchen towel to remove excess water. Stuff the capsicums with the corn filling and seal with the caps. Secure with a string each capsicum. Place in a casserole, dab with very little butter, and bake in hot oven till tender. Remove strings, and serve hot with garlic rolls or plain bread.

17. SPINACH-GREEN GRAM DELIGHT

Ingredients

½ cup green gram (whole), soaked for ½ hour
1 tsp lemon juice
½ inch ginger, grated
a few curry leaves
¼ tsp coriander powder
2 pinches asafoetida
¼ tsp mustard
salt to taste
1 bunch spinach, chopped finely
1 green chilli, slit lengthwise
2 flakes garlic, crushed
¼ tsp turmeric powder
¼ tsp chilli powder
¼ tsp cumin

Method

Boil the green gram till soft but not mushy. Add the spinach, and simmer, covered for two-three minutes. Remove from the fire. Heat oil in a deep pan, add the mustard and cumin. When they splutter, add the curry leaves, asafoetida, garlic, ginger and chilli, and stir-fry for a minute. Add all the other masalas, salt, 2 tbsps water, and stir well. Add the green gram-spinach, and stir gently. Serve hot, adding the lemon juice.

18. MALAI KOFTAS

Ingredients

- 200 gms spinach, chopped
- 1 tsp garam masala powder
- salt to taste
- 1 tsp turmeric powder
- 1 onions, chopped
- 4 tbsps cream, whipped
- oil for frying
- 200 gms cabbage, chopped
- 1 tsp rasam powder
- 1 tsp chilli powder
- 50 gms besan flour
- 2 tomatoes, chopped

Method

Puree the spinach and cabbage coarsely. Add the powders, salt and besan flour. Form balls and fry them until brown in colour. In a separate pan, heat the oil and fry the onions till pink. Then add the tomatoes and saute for another three minutes on medium heat. Now add the cream and salt, cook until the gravy thickens. Place the koftas in a serving dish. Pour the thick gravy over them, and serve hot.

19. AROMATIC CABBAGE

Ingredients

- 1 small cabbage, finely shredded
- 2 medium onions, chopped thinly

3 tbsps oil
½ tsp fennel
salt to taste
½ tsp cumin
4 tsps sesame

Method

Heat the oil in a pan. Add the cumin and fennel seeds. When they splutter, add the onions, and stir-fry for two-three minutes till the onions turn pink. Add the cabbage, stir-fry for a few seconds, cover the pan, and cook on low flame. Cook for two-three minutes or until the cabbage wilts. Uncover, and cook over high heat. Stir-fry for five minutes or until the cabbage gets tender.

20. CAPSICUM CURRY

Ingredients

½ kg capsicums
1 cup grated coconut
2 sprigs curry leaves
1 tsp cumin
2 tsps coriander seeds
1 tsp ginger paste
¼ kg roasted peanuts
1 pod garlic
2" cinnamon
5 tbsps oil
2 onions, chopped
coriander leaves

Method

Cut the capsicums lengthwise into four. Mix the peanuts, coconut, half the garlic, and blend them into a fine powder. Mix the coriander and cuminseeds, cinnamon, salt, onions, remaining garlic, and grind them to a fine paste. Heat the oil in a wide pan. Fry the onion mixture until brown. Sprinkle the fine peanut-coconut powder over the capsicums and add these to the onions. Sprinkle water if required, and cook on a low flame until the capsicum is tender. Remove from heat, and serve hot, garnished with curry and coriander.

21. MIXED VEGETABLE CURRY

Ingredients

250 gms cottage cheese, cubed into 2.5 cm pieces
4 tomatoes, chopped
oil for frying
4 onions, chopped
4 capsicums, chopped
12 mushrooms, halved and sauted

For the Marinade

50 tbsp oil
1 tsp pepper powder
salt to taste

For the Sauce

1 tbsp oil
2 spring curry leaves
½ cup grated coconut
¼ tsp turmeric powder
2 onions, sliced
3 green chillies, chopped
salt to taste

Method

Mix all the marinade ingredients, and apply on the chopped vegetables. Set aside for half an hour. Arrange the vegetable and peneer cubes on skewers. Grill them until golden brown. Heat oil in a pan. Add the onion and saute well. Add the curry leaves and green chillies. Fry for two minutes. And finally add the coconut, salt and turmeric powder. Add a little water and cook well. Remove from heat and strain the sauce. Pour this over the grilled vegetables, and serve hot with sauted mushrooms.

22. MUSHROOM BAHAR

Ingredients

500 gms mushrooms, sliced
100 gms onions, sliced
2 tomatoes, chopped finely
1 tsp chilli powder
60 ml oil
1 tsps ginger-garlic paste
1 tsp turmeric powder

salt to taste
2 tbsps chopped coriander leaves
½ tsp garam masala powder
4 green chillies, slit lengthwise
1 capsicum, slivered

Method

Heat the oil in a pan. Add the onions, ginger-garlic paste, and stir-fry until light brown. To this, add the tomatoes, turmeric powder, chilli powder, green chillies, salt and stir for 2-3 minutes. Also add the mushrooms, stir well, and add a little water if necessary. Simmer till done. Now add the capsicum and coriander leaves. Lower the heat and cook for two minutes. Sprinkle the garam masala over it and cook for another two minutes. Serve hot, garnished with coriander leaves and green chillies.

23. POTATO-MINT ROAST

Ingredients

6 potatoes, boiled peeled and halved
¼ cup finely chopped coriander leaves
½ tsp coriander powder
2 tbsps oil
¼ cup mint leaves, finely chopped
½ tsp cumin powder
¼ tsp chilli powder
salt and pepper to taste

Method

Mix the potaotes with the mint leaves, powder, salt and pepper, and marinate for an hour. Heat the oil in a pan, and fry the potatoes on low fire until golden. Garnish with coriander leaves.

24. SOYA KOFTA CURRY

Ingredients

100gms soya granules
2 green chillies, minced
salt to taste
oil for deep frying
½ cup boiled onion paste
3-4 tbsps tomato paste
1 tsp coriander powder
½ tsp garam masala powder
1 tsp red chilli powder
1 potato, boiled and mashed
a pinch of nutmeg powder
2 tbsps besan flour
1 bay leaf
2 tsps ginger-garlic paste
½ tsp turmeric powder
coriander leaves for garnishing

Method

Soak the soya granules in lukewarm water for 15 minutes. Squeeze to remove excess water. Mix them with the mashed potato, chillies, nutmeg powder and salt. Add besan, and form into koftas. Deep fry until crisp. Keep aside. In 2 tbsps hot oil, add the bay leaf and onion paste. Cook till oil starts separating. Add the ginger-garlic paste and tomato paste, and saute for half a minute. Add the powders and cook for another minute. Add water, garam masala, salt and the koftas. Cook till gravy is thick. Garnish with coriander leaves.

25. MASALA POTATOES

Ingredients

½ kg potatoes, cut into 4 cms fingers
1 tsp coriander powder
1 tbsps garam masala
2 tbsps oil
salt to taste
½ tbsp chili powder

Method

Soak the potato fingers in cold water for 5 minutes. Heat the oil in a pan. Add the coriander and chilli powders, and stir-fry for half a minute. Add the potato fingers and salt, and mix well. Transfer onto a greased plate and spread them well. Place them in an oven and bake at 450°F for 20 minutes. Turn them when you are halfway through. Serve hot with rice or chapatis.

26. SAAG PANEER

Ingredients

- 100 gms pottage cheese, cubed
- ½ tsp garam masala
- 2 large bunches spinach, chopped
- 2 cardamom seeds
- 2 bay leaves
- 1 tsp ginger-garlic paste
- salt to taste
- ½ tsp turmeric
- 1 tsp tomato puree
- 1 onion, chopped
- 1 cup whipped cream
- ¼ tsp cumin seeds
- 1 tsp coriander powder
- 1" cinnamon
- 2 cloves
- 1 tomato and capsicum, chopped
- 1 tsp cumin powder
- coriander leaves for garnishing

Method

Heat the oil in a saucepan. Saute the onion till light brown. Add the cuminseeds, cardamom, cinnamon, bay leaves, cloves, ginger-garlic, tomato and pepper, and saute for half a minute. Add the spinach, and stir-fry till it changes colour. When it becomes dark green, remaining crunchy, add the salt and the powders. Mix well. Add the cream, tomato puree, coriander leaves and cheese cubes. Cook well, stirring well. When the cream boils, cook for nearly two minutes.

27. MUGHLAI PALAK

Ingredients

- 1 kg spinach, chopped finely
- 4 tbsps oil
- 2" ginger, chopped
- 4 cardamoms
- 1 tsp garam masala
- salt to taste
- 4 tbsps butter
- 3 onions, chopped into fine half rings
- ¼ tsp fennel, crushed
- chilli powder to tste

Method

Heat the oil in a pan over medium-high flame. Add the fennel and cardamoms. Stir once or twice, then add the onions and ginger. Stir-fry until the onions turn a rice brown colour. Add the spinach. Cover and allow it to wilt completely, stirring every now and then. Turn the heat to medium, then add the salt and chilli powder. Cover and cook for 20-25 minutes. Remove the lid and add the garam masala, stir and cook uncovered for a further five minutes or until all the liquid has evaporated from the pan. Serve hot with naan, paratha, chapati or plain rice.

28. MATAR KEEMA

Ingredients

- ½ cup ghee
- 2 medium potatoes, finely chopped
- 2 medium tomatoes, chopped fine
- 1 tsp garam masala powder
- 1 tbsp grated ginger +1 tsp extra
- 1½ tsps coriander powder
- 2 cups peas, coarsely ground
- 1½ cup water
- 2 onions, chopped
- 2 bay leaves
- 6 cloves garlic, crushed
- 1½ tsps turmeric powder
- salt to taste
- chopped coriander leaves

Method

Mix together garlic, extra ginger, turmeric, chilli and coriander powders. Heat 1 tbsp ghee in a pan over low heat. Add the ginger (1 tbsp) and peas. Fry gently for five minutes until the grains of peas start to separate. Set aside. Add another tbsp of ghee to the pan, and fry for five minutes. Mix with the peas. Heat the remaining ghee. Add the bay leaves and onion, and fry till golden brown. Reduce the heat, and stir in the tomatoes and paste. Cook for 10 minutes, stirring occasionally. When the ghee starts to separate, add the peas-potatoes mixture with salt. Cook, for five minutes. Add the water, cover and simmer for 15 minutes. Serve hot, sprinkled with coriander leaves and garam masala.

29. BEETROOT-PEAS DELIGHT

Ingredients

- 2 beetroots, cubed
- ½ cup curd
- salt to taste
- ¼ cup peas
- 1 tsp rice flour

For the Gravy

- 1 onion
- 1" ginger
- 2 tsps poppy seeds
- ¼ cup coconut
- 4 green chillies
- 1 clove garlic
- 6-8 cashewnuts
- 3 stalks coriander leaves

Method

Boil the beetroot with peas and salt in a cup of water. Grind all the masala items for the gravy into a smooth paste. Combine the rice flour with the gravy thoroughly. Add to the vegetables, and stir to combine. Cook for five minutes. Add the curd, stir well and serve immediately.

30. PEAS MUSHROOM

Ingredients

1 cup peas
1 onion, chopped
coriander leaves for garnishing
1 tbsp oil
1 cup mushrooms, sliced
1 tomato, chopped
salt to taste

For the Gravy

¼ cup grated coconut
2 gloves garlic
1" cinnamon
2 green chillies
1" ginger

Method

Grind all the ingredients for the gravy into a smooth paste. Heat the oil in a pan. Fry the onion to a golden brown. Add the paste and stir-fry for a minute. Add the tomato, peas, mushrooms and salt. Cook for a minute. Add a cup of water, and simmer on a slow fire till done. Garnish with chopped coriander leaves, and serve hot.

31. PEARL ONIONS-PEAS IN CREAM SAUCE

Ingredients

20 baby onions, peeled
¾ cup curd
salt and pepper to taste
1 cup peas
1 tsp flour
1 tbsp oil

Method

Heat the oil in a pan. Add the onions, cook, covered, for five minutes. Stir in the peas, cover and cook for five minutes. Mix the flour with cream, and whisk slowly. Add to the peas-onion mixture. Add the salt and pepper, and cook till it reaches a sauce consistency. Serve hot.

32. PUMPKIN CURRY

Ingredients

½ kg pumpkin, diced
1 tsp grated ginger
¼ tsp cumin
salt and pepper to taste
1 green chilli, chopped
1 tbsp coriander powder
1 tbsp oil
coriander leaves for garnishing

Method

Heat the oil in a pan. Brown the chilli and splutter the cumin. Add all the other ingredients with half a glass of hot water. Cover and cook over a low heat util the pumpkin is tender and the water has been absorbed. Serve hot on a bed of rice and garnish with coriander leaves.

33. CUCUMBER-PEAS KURMA

Ingredients

3 cups diced cucumber
4 tbsps oil
2 cardamoms
1" piece cinnamon
½ cup chopped tomatoes
¼ tsp turmeric powder
coriander leaves, chopped
1 cup peas, boiled
1 tsp cuminseeds
2 cloves
½ cup chopped onions
½ cup curd, beaten
½ tsp chilli powder

For the Masala Paste (Grind)

4 green chillies
1 tbsp poppy seeds
¼ cup cashewnuts

Method

Heat the oil and add the cuminseeds. When they splutter, add the garam masala pieces. Saute for a minute. Add the onions and saute till light pink. Add the masala paste and saute till the oil separates. Add the tomato and cucumber pieces. Cover and cook on medium heat until tender. Add the beaten curd, turmeric, red chillies, peas and salt. Cook until the gravy is thick. Garnish with chopped coriander leaves and serve hot.

34. VEGETABLE DHANSAK

Ingredients

- 1 cup mixed lentils/legumes
- 2 cups mixed vegetable
- 1 small onion. chopped
- 1 green chilli, chopped
- 2 tsps garam masala powder
- 1 tbsp lemon juice
- 3 cups water
- 4 tbsps oil
- 2 cloves garlic, chopped
- ½ tsp turmeric powder
- salt to taste
- 3 tbsps chopped coriander leaves

Method

Soak the legumes for an hour. Place in a pan with water, and bring it to a boil. Add the vegetables and cook for 10 minutes. Heat oil in a separate pan. Saute the onion and garlic till golden brown. Stir in the chilli, turmeric and garam masala. Mix thoroughly. Add the legumes with oil, and stir well. Add the salt, and cook covered for 20 minutes until the lentils are soft. Add the lemon juice and coriander leaves, and serve hot.

35. VEGETABLE JALFREZI

Ingredients

- 3 cups boiled vegetables
- 2 spring onions, chopped
- ½" piece ginger, grated
- 1 cup tomato ketchup
- 1 tsp sugar
- salt to taste
- 2 onions, chopped
- 2 tomatoes, chopped
- 1 tbsp chopped coriander leaves
- 1 tsp chilli powder
- 3 tbsps ghee

Method

Heat the oil in a pan. Fry the onions till golden. Add the tomatoes, chillies, ginger and coriander, and saute for two minutes. Add the ketchup, boiled vegetables, spring onions, chilli powder, sugar, salt and a little water, and cook for about 10 minutes. Serve hot.

36. PANEER BUTTER-MASALA

Ingredients

- 1 cup peas
- 2 large tomatoes, chopped
- 1" ginger, grated
- ½ tsp coriander powder
- ¼ tsp turmeric powder
- 1 tps sugar
- 1 tsp chilli powder
- 3 tbsps oil
- 2 tsp tamarind pulp
- 2 tsps cream
- 2 carrots, chopped and boiled
- 100 gms cottage cheese, cubed
- 3 green chillies, chopped
- ½ tsp cumin powder
- 1 tsp garam masala powder

Method

Puree together the carrots, ginger, green chillies, tamarind and tomato. Boil the cheese with a little salt and a pinch of turmeric. Heat the oil in a pan. Add the carrot puree. Stir-fry for two minutes. Add the turmeric and the powders. Keep stirring till the oil separates. Add the cream salt and sugar, and stir-fry on low flame. Add the cheese and peas and a cup of water. Cook on low flame with the pan covered till the peas are cooked. Remove from the fire. Serve hot, garnished with coriander leaves and a blob of butter.

37. STUFFED TINDA IN CURD

Ingredients

500 gms tinda
2 tsps cumin-coriander powder
½ tsp chilli powder
2 tbsps oil
250 gms curd
¼ tsp turmeric powder
½ tsp pepper powder
salt to taste
¼ cup water

Method

Slit the tindas slightly. Mix the coriander-cumin, turmeric, chilli powder, salt and pepper. Stuff the tindas with this mixture. Heat oil in a pan. Add the curds, tindas and water. Transfer to a vessel and pressure cook for three minutes. Remove the vessel from the cooker and transfer its contents into the pan. Simmer on low heat till the oil separates form the curd and tindas.

38. LOTUS STEM CURRY

Ingredients

250 gms lotus stem, chopped
50 gms curd
½ tsp chilli powder
1" ginger, grated
salt to taste
4 cups water
150 gms potatoes, cut into small pieces
¼ tsp turmeric powder
¼ garam masala
3 green chillies, chopped
2 tbsps oil

Method

Pressure cook the lotus stem pieces in 2 cups of water. Heat oil and add the tomatoes, chillies and ginger. Saute till the oil separates. Add the lotus stem, potatoes, curd, turmeric and chilli powders. Keep stirring till the curd blends with the other masalas. Add salt and the remaining water. Cook on medium heat till the gravy is thick. Sprinkle garam masala powder over it and serve hot.

39. ARBI FRY

Ingredients

350gms arbi (colocasia), boiled and peeled
2 lemons
1 tsp garam masala powder
½ tsp chilli powder
oil for frying
salt to taste

Method

Mix salt and chilli powder in lime juice. Coat the arbi with this and marinate in the fridge for an hour. Heat the oil in a pan and deep fry the arbi. Serve hot, sprinked with the garam powder.

40. CAULIFLOWER CHEESE

Ingredients

1 large cauliflower, broken into florets
½ cup curd, whipped
1 cube cheese (50 gms), grated
1 bay leaf
½ tsp garam masala
salt to tastes
½ cup peas, boiled
2 tbsps chopped spring onion
oil for frying
½ tsp aniseed
¼ tsp turmeric powder

Grind to a Coarse Paste

3 large onions
7 red chillies
1" ginger

Grind with Milk

10 cashewnuts
1 tbsp poppy seeds (soaked in hot milk)

Method

Heat 1 tbsp oil in a pan. Add the bay leaf, aniseed, garam masala and the ground paste. Fry till oil separates from the masala. Add the cauliflower, a little water and turmeric powder. Cook till the cauliflower becomes soft. Add the cooked peas and curd, and cook till oil floats on top. Add the cashewnut paste, salt, a little sugar and a little milk, if necessary. Stir and simmer for two minutes, remove form the fire. Serve hot with grated cheese and spring onion.

LENTILS AND DALS

LENTILS AND DALS

1. EXOTIC SPICY DAL

Ingredients

- 100 gms urad dal (soaked for 8 hours)
- 2 tsps ginger-garlic paste
- 50 gms butter
- 1 tsp ajwain
- 1 tsp garam masala powder
- salt to taste
- 150 gms tomato puree
- 50 gms cream
- 2 tsps chilli powder
- 1 tsp kasoori methi powder

Method

Wash and boil the dal with salt and 1 tsp ginger-garlic paste. Simmer for nearly 2 hours over low heat. In a separate pan, heat the oil and add the rest of the ginger-garlic paste. Mix in the tomato puree. Cook for a few moments and add the boiled dal. Add the butter, cream and ajwain, chilli powder, garam masala and kasoori methi powders. Cook for 15 minutes. Serve hot.

2. SPINACH DAL

Ingredients

- 1 cup red gram, pressure-cooked
- ½ tsp bengal gram
- 1 tomato, chopped
- ½ tsp mustard
- 1 green chilli, slit lengthwise
- ½ tsp garam masala
- salt to taste
- 1 large bunch spinach, chopped
- ½ tsp black gram
- 1 tbsp oil
- 1 red chilli (broken into 2-3 bits)
- 4 curry leaves

Method

Heat the oil and add the mustard, the grams, red chilli and curry leaves. When the mustard splutters, add the spinach and half cup of water along with the green chilli. When the spinach is half cooked, add the tomato and garam masala. Saute for a minute, then add the red gram dal. Simmer on low heat till the spinach is cooked and the dal is not very watery. Serve hot with rice. Make sure that you don't overcook the spinach as then the nutrients will be lost.

3. CHANA IN TOMATO AND CURDS

Ingredients

- 6 firm tomatoes
- 2 tbsps bengal gram
- 1 tsp grated ginger
- 1 tsp chilli powder
- ¼ tsp turmeric powder
- ½ tsp garam masala powder
- ½ tsp clove-cinnamon powder
- 1 cup beaten curd
- 1 cup chana, soaked overnight
- salt to taste
- 1 tsp garlic paste
- 1 tsp cumin powder
- ½ tsp pepper powder
- ½ tsp amchoor powder
- 1 tbsp oil

- 1 onion, minced
- ½ tsp cumin powder
- 1 tbsp mint paste
- 1 tbsp tamarind juice
- 1 tbsp finely chopped coriander leaves
- 1 tbsp fine sev

Method

Snip off the top end of the tomatoes horizontally. Scoop out the pulp from them. Heat the oil, add the ginger-garlic and the scooped out pulp and juice of the tomatoes. Simmer for three minutes. Add all the masalas and mix well. Add the chana and simmer till the liquid is absorbed. Fill the tomatoes with this mixture. Bake in preheated oven, or steam in a colander for three minutes. Place them carefully in a serving dish. Mix the salt and cumin in curd. Pour this over the tomatoes. Pour the tamarind juice over it, spread the mint paste with a spoon on top of each tomato. Cover with minced onions, sev and coriander. Serve hot.

4. CURD-GREEN GRAM RELISH

Ingredients

- 1 cup sprouted green gram, cooked
- 3 tbsps sweet chutney
- 3 tbsps sev
- ¼ cup chopped tomatoes
- 2 tbsps minced onion
- salt to taste
- chilli powder to taste
- 1 cup curd, beaten
- 2 tbsps green chutney
- coriander leaves for garnishing
- 1 green chilli, minced
- 1 potato, boiled and mashed coarsely

Method

Spread the dal in a serving bowl. Top it with the potato. Add the salt and chilli powder. Spread the curd over it. Top this with tomatoes, onion, green chutney, and sweet chutney. Garnish with coriander and sev.

5. DAL MAKHANI

Ingredients

- ½ cup red gram, soaked
- ¼ cup masoor dal, soaked
- 2 green chillies, chopped
- ½ tbsp finely chopped coriander leaves
- ½ tsp chilli powder
- salt to taste
- ¼ cup split green gram, soaked
- 1 onion, minced
- ¼ tsp grated ginger
- ½ tsp cumin powder
- 3 tbsps butter

Method

Pressure cook the dal till soft but not overcooked. Mash a quarter of it while hot. Heat the butter in a pan. Add the cumin and allow them to splutter. Add the onion, ginger and chillies. Stir-fry till soft. Add the chilli powder, dals and salt. Stir well and bring it to a boil. Simmer for three or four minutes. Garnish with coriander leaves. (You can squeeze a lemon over it if you want.)

6. CHANA-MOONG COMBINE

Ingredients

- ½ cup green gram, soaked for an hour
- 1 tsp chilli powder
- ½ tsp garam masala powder
- ¼ tsp coriander powder
- ½ lemon
- ½" ginger, grated
- ½ tsp mustard
- ½ cup chana, soaked overnight
- 1 tbsp ghee
- ¼ tsp turmeric powder
- salt to taste
- 1 tbsp chopped coriander leaves
- ½ tsp cumin

Method

Pressure cook the chana and green gram separately. Mix all the spice powders in half cup of water to make a thin paste.

Heat the ghee in a pan. Splutter the mustard and cumin. Add the thin paste. Saute for a minute, then add the dal and chana. Add enough water to cover the mixture. Bring to a bowl. Add the salt. When the gravy is thick, add the lemon juice. Serve hot, garnished with coriander.

7. DOODHI DAL

Ingredients

- 1 small bottlegourd, chopped
- 1 tsp chopped coriander leaves
- ¾ tsp corianssder powder
- ¼ tsp turmeric powder
- ½ tsp sugar
- a pinch of asafoetida
- ½ cup bengal gram, soaked for 20 minutes
- ½ tsp chilli powder
- 1 tbsp oil
- 4 curry leaves
- ½ cup water
- salt to taste
- 1 tsp tamarind pulp

Method

Mix all the dry masalas in the water. Heat the oil in a pan. Add the mustard and cumin, and when they splutter, add the curry leaves, asafoetida and masala water. Simmer for two minutes. Add the dal, and gourd and cook for 10 minutes till dal is tender. Add the sugar, tamarind, salt and cook for two more minutes. Garnish with coriander leaves.

8. CHOLAR DAL

Ingredients

- 1 cup bengal gram
- 1 tsp cumin
- 5 cm cinnamon
- 2 red chillies, halved
- 1 tsp chilli powder
- 1 tsp sugar
- salt to taste
- 2 tbsps ghee
- 4 cardamoms
- 2 bay leaves
- ¼ cup finely chopped coconut slices
- ½ tsp cumin powder

Method

Cook the dal with four cups of water till soft. Heat the ghee in a pan. Season with cumin, cardamom, cinnamon and bay leaves. Add the chillies and coconut slices. Saute till coconut is light brown. Add all the powders, mix well. Then add the dal, salt and sugar, and simmer for five minutes. Serve hot.

9. TOMATO DAL

Ingredients

- 1 cup red gram, cooked
- ¾ cup chopped onions
- 1 tbsp oil
- 1 tsp cumin
- 4 curry leaves
- salt to taste
- ¼ tomatoes, chopped
- 2 green chillies, chopped
- ½ tsp mustard
- 1 tsp black gram
- 1 tsp chilli powder

Method

Heat the oil in a pan. Add the mustard and cumin. When they splutter, add the curry leaves, onions and green chillies. Fry till the onions are light pink. Add the tomatoes, cook covered on a low flame till the vegetables are soft. Add the chilli powder, dal, salt and water (if necessary). Simmer for five minutes. Serve hot with rice or chapati.

10. MASOOR DAL EXOTICA

Ingredients

- 2 cups masoor dal, boiled and cooked
- 1 tsp turmeric powder
- 2 tbsps oil
- 1 clove garlic, minced
- 1 tsp garam masala powder
- salt to taste
- 1 large onion, chopped
- 1" ginger, grated

2 green chillies, chopped
1 bunch coriander leaves, chopped
2 tomatoes, chopped

Method

Heat the oil in a pan. Add the onions and saute till just pink. Add the garlic, ginger and chillies. Saute till onion turns golden brown. Add the powders and stir-fry for a minute. Add the tomatoes and coriander leaves. Stir-fry till the tomatoes soften. Pour in the dal and add the salt. Simmer for about five minutes till the dal becomes thick. Garnish with coriander leaves. Serve hot.

11. LOBHIA

Ingredients

1½ cups black-eyed beans (lobhia) (soaked overnight)
1 small onion, chopped
½ tsp turmeric powder
1" ginger, grated
1 tomato, chopped
salt to taste
¾ tsp cumin powder
1 tsp coriander powder
2 tbsps oil
½ tsp cuminseeds

Method

Boil the lobhias with salt, and the spice powders. Simmer till the beans (lobhia) are tender. Heat the oil in a pan. Add the onion, garlic, ginger and cumin. Saute for 10 minutes. Add the lobhia, and simmer, uncovered, until they are soft but not mushy. Serve hot.

12. FIVE-JEWEL CREAMED LENTILS

Ingredients

175 gms bengal gram
45 gms green gram
45 gms red gram
90 gms black gram
45 gms masoor dal
½ tsp turmeric

salt to taste
2 onions, sliced in rings
2 tsps ginger paste
2 tsps cumin
1 tsp paprika
2 green chillies, minced
6 tbsps oil
2 tsps garlic paste
3 tomatoes, cut into 2 cm wedges
½ tsp pepper
2 tbsps chopped coriander

Method

Boil all the five dals with turmeric. Add the salt. Heat the oil in a pan. Fry the onions till light brow. Add the garlic, ginger and chillies, and saute for two more minutes. Add the tomatoes and saute for about five minutes. Add the dal and stir for a minute. Season with cumin, pepper and paprika. Stir for a couple of minutes. Remove from the fire and serve, garnished with coriander.

13. KALI DAL

Ingredients

1 cup split black gram
½ turmeric powder
½ tsp cumin powder
3 green chillies, chopped
salt to taste
1 red chilli (whole)
1 tsp chilli powder
½ tsp coriander powder
5 cloves garlic, minced
½ tsp sugar

Method

In a hot pan, dry roast the dal. Add five cups of water and all the ingredients except garlic and whole red chilli. Cook till the dal is tender. Heat the oil and fry the whole red chilli till brown. Add the garlic and saute till it turns brown. Add the dal, and simmer for five minutes. Serve hot.

14. DAL MAHARANI

Ingredients

- 100 gms rajma (soaked overnight)
- 50 gms bengal gram
- ½ tsp coriander powder
- ½ tsp chilli powder
- 2 onions, chopped
- ½ tsp ginger-garlic paste
- 2 tbsps oil
- 50 gms black gram
- salt to taste
- 2 tomatoes, chopped
- ½ tsp garam masala powder
- ¼ tsp turmeric powder
- 1 tbsp butter
- 2 green chillies, chopped

Method

Pressure cook the rajma with the dals and turmeric powder. Heat the oil in a pan. Fry the onions till pink. Add the ginger-garlic paste. Saute for a minute. Add the tomatoes and fry for two minutes. Add the powders, chillies and a little water. Cook for a minute. Add the rajma, and simmer for about eight minutes. Serve hot with the butter on it.

15. KHATTA CHANNA

Ingredients

- 250 bengal gram (whole), soaked overnight
- 2 onions, chopped
- 1" ginger, grated
- salt to taste
- 1 tsp roasted cuminseeds
- 2 tbsps oil
- ½ cup tamarind pulp
- 4 tomatoes, chopped
- 1 tbsp chana masala powder
- 1 tsp chilli powder
- 1 tsp coriander powder
- coriander leaves, chopped

Method

Pressure cook the chana with salt. Heat the oil in a pan. Add the cumin, coriander powder, chana masala and chilli powder, and salt. Saute for two minutes. Add the ginger, onions, green chillies and tomatoes, and saute for three minutes. Add the tamarind juice and cook for five minutes on medium heat. Remove from the fire. Garnish with onion and tomato slices and coriander leaves.

16. CHANA-PANEER

Ingredients

- 150 gms bengal gram, soaked for 2 hours
- 2 onions, chopped
- 2" cinnamon
- 4 cloves
- 1 whole red chilli
- ¼ tsp chilli powder
- 1" ginger, grated
- 2 tbsps oil
- 200 gms cottage cheese, cubed
- 2 tomatoes, chopped
- 2 cardamoms
- 2 bay leaves
- ¼ tsp turmeric powder
- few sprigs of coriander
- 3 flakes garlic, minced
- salt to taste

Method

Heat the oil in a pan. Fry the onions till light brown. Add the ginger, garlic, cinnamon, cardamoms, cloves, bay leaves and chilli. Add the tomatoes and saute till the oil separates. Add the dal, salt, and the powders, and saute for six minutes. Pour nearly two cups of water. Pressure cook till the dal is cooked. Remove from the cooker, and boil in the pan for five minutes. Serve hot.

17. DAL FRY

Ingredients

- 1 cup black gram, soaked for 2 hours
- 5 cloves garlic, minced
- ½ cumin
- 1" ginger, grated
- 2 green chillies chopped
- 1 tsp garam masala

1 tbsp coriander powder
1 tsp chilli powder
¼ cup finely chopped onion
1 tbsp oil
1 tbsp cream
1 lemon
powder
1 tsp cumin powder
salt to taste
2 tomatoes, chopped
1 tbsp chopped coriander leaves

Method

Pressure cook the dal with ginger and garlic. Mash the dal slightly. Heat the oil in a pan. Add the cumin, chillies and then onion. Fry till crisp. Add the tomatoes and stir for a minute. Add the powders and salt. Mix well. Add the dal and cook for a five minutes. Remove from heat. Squeeze lemon juice into the dal. Decorate with whipped cream and coriander leaves.

18. BAKED SOYA BEANS

Ingredients

1 cup soya beans, soaked for 8 hours
1 cheese cube, grated
2 green chillies, slit
¾ cup tomato puree
3 tbsp tomato sauce
salt to taste
2 tsps sugar
1 tsp chilli powder
2 tbsps butter
½ tsp garam masala
1 tbsp chopped coriander
1 tsp coriander powder
1 tbsp cornflour
1 tbsp vinegar
¼ tsp pepper

Method

Mix together all the ingredients from tomato puree to chilli powder. Pressure cook the beans till they done. Strain and mix the beans with butter, cheese, green chillies, and coriander leaves, and the tomato puree mixture. Blend thoroughly. Garnish with slit chillies and coriander, sprinkling garam masala powder on top.

19. SAMBHAR

Ingredients

2 cups red gram
2 onions, chopped
½ tsp fenugreek
½ tsp turmeric powder
6-8 red chillies
salt to taste
6 curry leaves
lemon-size tamarind ball
1 cup vegetables, chopped and boiled
2 tbsps coriander seeds
a pinch of asafoetida
2 tbsps coconut gratings
2 tbsps oil
1 tsp mustard
2 tbsps chopped coriander

Method

Pressure cook the dal with turmeric. Mash the dal till it is pasty. Lightly fry the onion. Add the vegetables and stir fry for a minute. Deep aside. Heat the oil in a pan. Fry the coriander seeds, fenugreek, asafoetida and chillies. Grind this with coconut. Keep aside. Boil the onion-vegetable mixture, untill the onion is cooked. Add the tamarind extract and salt. Cook for five minutes. Add the spice paste. Boil for a minute, then add the dal. Simmer for a minute. Season with mustard and curry leaves. Garnish with the coriander leaves.

SNACKS

SNACKS

1. ARBI AMRITSARI

Ingredients

300 gms arbi
30 gms cornflour
salt to taste
1 tsp ajwain
2 tsps ginger-galic paste
50 gms besan
50 gms breadcrumbs
1 tsp chilli powder
1 tsp cumin powder
oil for frying

Method

Boil and skin the arbi. Flatten each of the arbi and set aside. Dry roast the besan till golden brown. Add the cornflour, breadcrumbs, salt, chilli powder, ajwain, cumin powder and ginger-garlic paste. Coat the arbi with this mixture. Deep fry all the coated arbis till golden brown. Serve hot with sauce.

2. CAULIFLOWER PAKORAS

Ingredients

1 small cauliflower
1 cup tomato sauce
1 tsp chilli, powder
a pinch of soda
salt to taste
oil for frying
1 tbsp chaat masala
1 cup besan
1 tsp ajwain
1 tsp ginger-green chilli paste

Method

Separate the florets from the stalk and wash them very well. Put them an absorbed paper till water is absorbed. Sprinkle chaat masala on top. Mix in the tomato sauce and leave for half an hour. Prepare a smooth batter with the besan and fry in hot oil till crisp and golden. Serve hot with spicy chutney.

3. HARA BHARA KABAB

Ingredients

- 4 potatoes, boiled and grated
- 1 bunch spinach
- 2 tbsps chopped coriander
- salt to taste
- 2 tbsps cornflour
- oil for deep frying
- ¾ cup peas, boiled and mashed
- 1 tsp chaat masala
- 1 tbsp chopped green chillies
- 1 tbsp chopped ginger

Method

Blanch the spinach in plenty of salted boiling water. Remove and dip in cold water. Squeeze out excess water, and chop finely. Mix the spinach with potatoes and peas. Add the chillies, coriander, ginger, chaat masala and salt. Add the cornflour for binding. Divide into 25 equal portions into balls and shape into tikkis. Heat the oil in a deep pan. Deep fry the kababs till golden brown. Remove onto a tissue paper to absorb excess oil. Serve hot with chutney.

4. DAHIVADA

Ingredients

- 1 cup split black gram, soaked for 1 hour
- 1 tbsp peppercorns, crushed
- salt to taste
- 2 tsps grated ginger
- 2 tbsps coconut gratings
- 1 tbsp mix flour

For the Dahi Mixture

½ tsp mustard
1 bunch coriander, finely chopped
2 cups curds
1 tsp sugar
¼ tsp cumin
1 green chilli, finely chopped
salt to taste

Method

Mix all the ingredients for the vada, and grind into a thick paste. Take a lime-size portion of this batter in your hand, form into a ball, flatten and deep fry. Use up all the batter to fry the vadas. When the vadas are golden brown and crisp, remove them from the oil and immense them in hot salted water for two minutes. Remove from the water and lay them in a serving bowl. Heat 1 tsp oil in a pan. Fry the mustard, cumin and chilli. Season the curd with this. Add the salt and sugar and mix well. Pour over the vada to cover them completely. Garnish with coriander leaves.

5. ALOO BONDA

Ingredients

½ kg potatoes, boiled and mashed
1 bunch coriander, finely chopped
salt to taste
oil for frying
2 small onions, chopped
4 green chillies, chopped finely
1 tsp grated ginger

For the batter

1 cup besan flour
1 tbsps rice flour
salt to taste
a pinch of asafoetida
½ tsp ajwain
1 tsp chilli powder

Method

Prepare the batter by mixing all the ingredients in water into a thick consistency. Mix all the ingredients for the bondas and form into lemon-size balls. Dip these balls in the batter and deep fry till it has a rich brown colour. Remove onto a tissue paper, and serve hot with ketchup.

6. PANEER TIKKA

Ingredients

- 400gms cottage cheese, 3 cm slabs
- 2 tsp chopped coriander
- 8 clove garlic
- 2 tsps lemon juice
- 1 tsp chilli powder
- 2 tbsps oil
- 2 tsp chopped mint leaves
- a pinch of ajwain
- 2 tsps ginger paste
- 1 tsp garam masala powder
- salt and pepper to taste

Method

Make a paste of garlic, ajwain and coriander leaves. Mix with ginger paste. Add all the other ingredients except the cheese and oil. Marinate the cheese slabs with this mixture, and keep aside for an hour. Apply a little oil on each cheese, and bake till the tikkas are golden brown. Serve hot.

7. INSTANT DHOKLAS

Ingredients

- 1 cup semolina
- 1 cup curd
- ½ tsp sugar
- ½ tsp mustard
- 6 red chillies
- a pinch of asafoetida
- salt to taste
- 1 tsp green chilli-ginger paste
- 1 tsp Eno fruit salts
- 1 tsp sesame
- 2 tbsps oil
- 1 sprig coriander, chopped

Method

In a bowl, mix the semolina, salt, paste, and sugar. Add the curd to semolina, and mix well, the consistency being that of idli batter. Add the Eno salt and mix thoroughly. Pour this onto a greased flat plate. In a skillet boil three glasses of water. Place a small cup in the centre and place the plate containing the batter over the cup. Close the container and steam for 15 minutes. Remove the plate from the skillet and cool. Heat the oil in a pan. Add the mustard. When it splutters, add the red chillies, sesame and asafoetida. Pour onto the dhokla. Garnish with coriander, and cut into squares.

8. BHELPURI

Ingredients

- ½ cup puffed rice
- ½ cup chopped onions
- 2 chillies, chopped
- 2 tbsps lemon juice
- ½ tsp black salt
- ½ cup sev
- ½ cup freed dal mixture
- ½ cup tamarind chutney
- 3 potatoes, boiled and cubed

Method

Spread the puffed rice on a plate. Top it up with sev. Sprinkle a layer of onions over it followed by the dal mixture. Layer this with potatoes. Sprinkle chilli powder, black salt and green chillies over it. Pour tamarind chutney over this and serve.

Variation

Mix all the ingredients in a bowl and then serve.

9. VEGETABLE CUTLETS

Ingredients

- 1 cup cooked vegetables
- 2 green chillies, chopped
- 1 potato, boiled and mashed

½ tsp ginger-garlic paste
salt to taste
oil for frying
½ cup breadcrumbs
½ tsp cornflour

Method

Add all the ingredients except oil and bread to the potatoes. Make into cutlets and roll in the breadcrumbs. Heat the oil in a pan, and fry the cutlets until golden brown on both sides. Serve with any sauce.

10. NAMAK PARAS

Ingredients

2 cups maida (or wheat flour)
½ cup warm water
½ teaspoon kalonji
2 tbsps oil
½ tsp salt
oil to fry

Method

Make the dough by adding 2 tbsps oil, salt, kalonji and warm water to the flour. Roll out the dough not very thin. Cut strips diagonally and then cut diagonally in the opposite direction to shape and diamonds. Heat the oil in a pan and deep fry the paras till they are golden and crisp.

11. PAPRI CHAAT

Ingredients

1½ cups wheat flour
¼ cup oil
½ tsp turmeric powder
1 tsp cumin, crushed
2 tsps ghee or vegetable oil
2 potatoes, boiled and mashed
3 cups maida
1 tsp chilli powder
¼ tsp asafoetida
1 tsp ajwain, crushed
salt to taste
2 tbsps green chutney
2 tbsps red chutney

Curd Mix

2 cups curd
2 curry leaves
¼ tsp cumin
2 tsps oil
2 tbsps sugar
¼ tsp mustard
salt to taste

Method

For the puris, mix together the maida, wheat flour, chilli powder. turmeric, salt, asafoetida, oil, cumin and ajwain. Add water and knead to a hard dough. Roll out small puris (3 cms in diameter) with the dough, prick with a fork. Deep fry and keep aside. For the curd mix, beat the curd and add sugar and salt to it. Season it with mustard, cumin and curry leaves. Mix thoroughly. To serve, crush the puris a little and place in the serving plate. Mix salt with the potatoes and layer over the puris. Pour 3 tbsps of curd mix over this, then 1 tsp of green chutney followed by 1 tsp of red chutney. Sprinkle chilli and chaat powder over this, and serve.

12. VEGETABLE SAMOSAS

Ingredients

1 large potato, chopped finely
1 cup lentils
2 tbsps oil
1 tsp cumin
1 tsp chilli powder
1 tbsp flour
3 tbsps oil
oil for deep frying
1 cup peas
1 onion, chopped finely
1 clove garlic, crushed
1 tbsp curry powder
1 cup water + ¼ cup extra
3 cups maida
1 cup warm water

Method

Heat the 2 tbsps oil in a pan and fry together the onion, garlic, curry powder, cumin and chilli powder for a minute. Add the lentils and cook for two minutes. Add the potatoes, peas and 1 cup water, and bring to a boil. Reduce the heat and simmer, covered, for 20 minutes or till the potatoes are tender. Blend the 1 tbsp flour using the ¼ cup water, and add to the boiling mixture. When the mixture thickens, remove form the fore and cool. To make the dough, mix the 3 tbsps oil with the maida, add the cumin, and gradually stir in the warm water with a little salt to form a fairly stiff dough. Cover, and let stand for half an hour. Divide the dough in half. Roll out each to 3 mm (1/8) thickness. Cut into round using 3.5 inches (9 cm) cutter. Place 1 tsp of filling in the centre of each round. Brush edges lightly with water, and fold in half, or in the form of samosas (triangular). Press edges with thumb and finger. Deep fry the samosas to a golden brown. Drain on paper towel. Serve with mint chutney.

13. MASALA VADA

Ingredients

- 2 cups bengal gram, soaked for an hour
- 8 green chillies
- 6 small onions, chopped finely
- 1 spring coriander, chopped finely
- 6 red chillies
- 1 tsp cumin
- 2 stalks curry leaves
- 1 bunch mint, chopped finely
- oil for deep frying
- salt to taste

Method

Grind together the dal, chillies and cumin to a fairly coarse texture. Add the salt, curry leaves, mint, and coriander. Shape into balls. Heat the oil in a pan, flatten the balls and deep fry to a rich brown colour and crispness. Serve hot with any chutney.

PUDDINGS AND DESSERTS

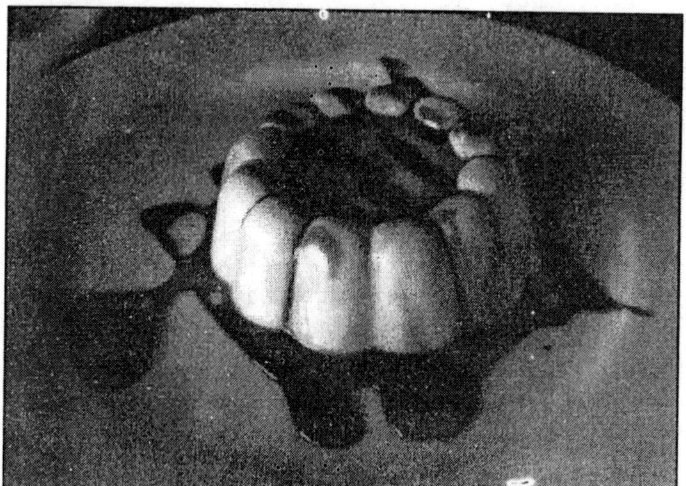

PUDDINGS AND DESSERTS

1. PHIRNI

Ingredients

¼ cup basmati rice
1½ cups sugar
4 cups milk
2-3 drops of rose water

For the Garnish

4 tsps almonds, blanched, skimmed and slivered
1 tsp cardamom powder

Method

Wash the rice and soak it for 30 minutes. Drain, put in a blender with 2 tbsps water and grind to a fine paste. Bring the milk to a boil in a pan. Add the rice paste and sugar, and stir with a whisk. On a low heat, cook, and stir with a whisk. On a low heat, cook, stirring continuously so that no lumps are formed. When the mixture becomes thick, add the rose water, stir and remove. Pour into small glass bowls. Garnish with cardamom powder and almond slivers. Cool and refrigerate until set. Serve cold.

2. KULFI

Ingredients

4 cups full-cream milk
1 tsp cardamom powder
2 tbsps cornflour
4 tbsps pistachios, blanched, skinned and slivered
1 tin condensed milk
½ tsp saffron, soaked in
2 tbsps warm milk
2 tsps kewra water

Method

In a thick-bottomed pan, bring the milk to a boil. Add the condensed milk. Lower the heat and let it simmer, stirring constantly. Add the cardamom powder and then stir every five minutes. After 20-25 minutes. When the mixture gets thicker, add the cornflour (dissolved in a little water), stirring continuously to avoid lumps. Continue cooking till the mixture is reduced to a custard consistency. Remove from the flame, add the saffron, pistachios and kewra water. Let the kulfi cool completely. Whisk the mixture, fill into kulfi moulds, and chill in the freezer for 5-6 hours. Remove from the freezer 5 minutes before serving. Demould and serve chilled.

3. LITCHI COOKIE DESSERT

Ingredients

150 ml litchi juice
2 cups butter cookie crumbs

For Garnishing

tutti frutti of dry fruits

Method

Heat the litchi juice in a thick-bottomed pan till lukewarm. Slow add the cookie crumbs, stirring continuously so that it does not stick to the bottom of the pan (2-3 minutes should do).

Pour the mixture into various shaped moulds. When at room temperature, spread the tutti frutti pieces over them. keep in the fridge for an hour. Unmould and serve.

4. CRUSTY SOUFFLE

Ingredients

1 litre milk
3-4 drops vanilla essence
4 tbsps gelatine
sugar to taste
2 cups cookie crumbs
4 tbsps butter

Method

Mix the butter and cookie crumbs with your fingers. Line the bottom of 2-3 inch mould with the cookie crumbs. Keep in the fridge for an hour till the crumbs are firm. Soak the gelatin in lukewarm water for 15 minutes. Boil the milk in a thick-bottomed pan and cook till reduced to one-fourth of its original quantity. Mix in the sugar and stir till the sugar melts. Mix in the essence and gelatine. Blend in a mixie so that the gelatin has mixed well into the milk. Pour into the moulds with the crumbs at the base. Return to the fridge and allow to set. When firm, loosen the sides of the souffle with the top of the knife. Place a plate on the mould and carefully turn over the souffle so that the crusty portion is on top.

5. FRUIT SUNDAE

Ingredients

200 gms fruits (strawberries, sapota, pineapple, banana)
50 gms powdered sugar
1 cup curds
½ cup cream

Method

Mix the sugar in the curd and stir till sugar dissolves. Add the chopped fruits. Pour into serving glasses or cups and top wit dollops of cream.

6. GAJAR KA HALWA

Ingredients

1½ kgs carrots, grated
200 gms condensed milk
½ cup cashewnuts, almonds and raisins
1 cup milk
2 tbsps ghee
1 tsp cardamom powder

Method

Pressure cook the grated carrots with milk. On a medium flame, cook till the water evaporates, stirring constantly so that it does not get burnt at the bottom. Pour the condensed milk and ghee and keep stirring over low flame till it is semi-dry and the condensed milk and ghee are well blended with the carrot. Remove from fire. Lightly fry the cashews and raisins, and these with the almonds to the halwa. Serve hot or chilled.

7. BESAN KA HALWA

Ingredients

1 cup besan flour
¾ cup sugar
½ cup ghee
1 cup milk
1 tsp cardamom powder
15 cashewnuts, finely chopped

Method

Heat the ghee in a pan. Add the besan flour and stir on low flame until the flour turns golden. Add the milk, sugar and cardamom. Keep on stirring the mixture until the mixture turms thick. Serve hot, garnished with fried cashews.

8. MANGO RABRI

Ingredients

6 cups milk
1 cup mango pulp
1 cup sugar

Method

Heat the milk in a pan. Simmer for an hour more till it has a granular consistency. Remove from the fire, and add the sugar. Stir till the sugar dissolves. Cool and add the mango pulp. Mix well and serve chilled.

9. RICE KHEER

Ingredients

- 1 lt milk
- 4 tbsps sugar
- ¼ cup cashewnuts and almonds, slivered
- ¼ cup rice
- ½ tsp cardamom powder
- 2 tbsps raisins, soaked in water

Method

Boil milk in a heavy pan. Add the rice and cook till the rice is cooked. Lower the flame, and simmer till it becomes thick and creamy. Add the nuts and cook for five more minutes. Chill and serve.

10. SUJI KA HALWA

Ingredients

- ½ cup semolina
- ¼ cup ghee
- ¼ tsp cardamom powder
- 1 tbsp raisins, fried
- 1 tbsp cashewnuts, fried
- ¼ cup sugar
- 1 cup water
- a pinch of red colouring powder (kesar)

Method

Fry the semolina in a dry pan till it becomes golden. Keep aside. Boil the water, and add the colour and semolina. Lower the heat, close the pan for a minute. Then stir well and ensure that there are no uncooked lumps. Add the sugar and stir till it melts. Then add the ghee gradually, stirring all the while. After five minutes, remove form the fine. Add the cardamom and dry fruits. Stir well and serve hot or chilled.

11. CHOCOLATE PUDDING

Ingredients

- 1 cup maida
- 2 tbsps raisins
- 100 gms butter
- 3 tbsps cashew, almonds, pista
- ½ tsp nutmeg-clove-cinnamon powder
- ¼ grated carrots
- 2 tbsps chopped dates
- 1 tsp powdered sugar
- ¾ tsp cooking soda
- 1 tsp rum
- a pinch of salt

For the Sauce

- ¼ cup sugar
- 1 cup milk
- 1 tsp butter
- 1 tbsp cornflour
- 1 tbsps cocoa powder

Method

Make the sauce by mixing together sugar, cornflour, salt, cocoa and milk. Cook on medium heat, stirring constantly. When it turns shiny, remove from the fire and add the butter. Keep aside. Cream the butter and sugar in a bowl until fluffy. Add the carrots, raisins and dates, and mix well. Add the essence, maida, salt soda and powdered spices little by little, stirring gently (do not over-beat). Add the nuts and stir. Apply butter to the pudding basin and fill it with the pudding mixture. Place this in a pressure cook, and steam for 1½ hours in medium flame. Serve hot with chocolate sauce and spread the rum essence with a spoon over the sauce.

12. BREAD APPLE PUDDING

Ingredients

- 9 slices bread, cut into fingers (crust removed)
- 3 tbsps butter
- ¼ cup cinnamon powder
- 1½ tbsps apple jam
- 2 apples
- ½ cup fresh breadcrumbs
- ½ cup powdered sugar
- 1½ tbsps butter (for apple pulp)

Method

Apply butter on the bread fingers and toast them on a hot tawa until golden brown. Peel the apples, remove the core and slice them. Pour a little water and cook until soft. Add the butter to the apples, and when it melts, remove from the fire. Mash and add to it the sugar, breadcrumbs, apple pulp, jam and cinnamon. In a greased pudding mould lay a bed of bread fingers closely together, slightly overlapping each other. Pour the apple mixture in the middle. Cover the top with the rest of the toasted finger slices. Cover the mould with a greaseproof paper, and tie it with string. Steam for 10 minutes in a pressure pan. When cool, unmould, and decorate with whipped cream and nuts. Chill and serve with more cream.

13. BASUNDI

Ingredients

- 8 cups milk
- ½ cup sugar
- a pinch of nutmeg powder
- 2 tsps chopped pistachios
- a few strands saffron
- 2 tsps coarsely ground almonds

Method

Boil the milk with saffron, stirring continously, until it reduces by half. Add the sugar, almonds and continue to cook until quite thick, but not dry. Stir in the pistachios.

14. BADAM PURI

Ingredients

2 cups plain flour
5 tbsps rice flour
2 cardamoms, powdered
1 cup sugar
6 tbsps butter
2 strands saffron
oil for deep frying
½ cup water

Method

In a bowl, mix the flour with 2 tbsps butter till the mixture is grandular. Add water gradually to make into a pliable dough. Cover with a damp cloth and set aside. Cream the remaining butter with the rice flour until creamy. Form 6-8 balls of the dough. Roll out another ball and place this on the first. Spread rice cream over this. Roll up slowly, tucking in the edges on either side. Cut into three or four slices and seal the spiral edges by twisting from left to right. Roll out to 1/8 inch thickness and deep fry until golden and crisp. Drain well on a paper towel. Make a thick syrup with sugar and water. Add the saffron, cardamom powder, and soak the puris in it for five minutes. Remove and dry on serving plate.

15. CHERRY PUDDING

Ingredients

2 cups tinned cherries
1 cup cherry syrup from the tin
½ tin condensed milk
¾ cup chilled water
½ cup powdered sugar
a few glaced cherries
3 tbsps gelatine
1 tsp vanilla essence
½ cup thick cream
½ cup grated coconut
1 tbsp lemon juice

Method

Mix the gelatine in the cherry syurp. Allow to soften. Heat the mixture till the gelatine dissolves. Remove and add the essence and cherries. Cool in the fridge till semi-it. Beat together the condensed milk and chilled water. Add the sugar and lemon juice. Add this to the cherry mixture. Add the coconut and stir well. Refrigerate till set. Decorate with whipped cream and glaced cherries.

16. STRAWBERRY RELISH

Ingredients

30 gms in gelatine, dissolved
2 cups milk
1 cup sugar
½ cup strawberries
12 Marie biscuts
3 tbsps custard powder
2 cups fresh cream
1 packet strawberry jelly
1 tsp vanilla essence

Method

Mix together the milk, custard powder and sugar. Heat till done. Mix the essence and cool. Prepare the jelly as given on the packet. Whip the cream with powdered sugar until stuff. Fold into the custard. In a transparent bowl, spread half the custard and over it half the jelly. Spread the bisciuts over the jelly. Cover with strawberries followed by the remaining custard. Spoon cream on top and serve chilled.

17. CARAMEL SOUFFLE

Ingredients

30 gms gelatine
1½ cups cream
10 gms almonds
275 ml milk
vanilla essence
250 gms sugar
10 gms cashewnuts

Method

Caramelise the sugar until brown and add nuts to it, cool and crush. Deep aside. Dissolve gelatine in ¼ cup warm water.

Add the sugar and mix well. Beat the cream till thick. Add the vanilla essence. Keep the cream aside. Mix the gelatine, sugar mixtue with milk and allow to set in the fridge and let it set. Before serving, spoon the cream over the souffle and decorate with the nuts.

18. MALPUA

Ingredients

½ tin milkmaid
50 gms maida
1 cup water
oil for frying
3 cups water
100 gms semolina
50 gms cottage cheese
10 almonds, slivered
1½ cups sugar
½ tsp cardamom powder

Method

Make a thick syrup with sugar and 3 cups water. Keep aside. Mix together the Milkmaid, semolina, maida, 1 cup water and baking powder. Set aside for half an hour. Crumble the cheese and add to the milkmaid. Heat the oil in a pan. Pour a ladle of the milkmaid batter to make a small malpua. Fry on both sides till brown and crisp. Strain the oil and immense in the sugar for a minute. Remove and keep in a plate. Fry all the malpuas thus, and decorate them with slivered almonds, sprinkling the cardamom powder over them.

19. PISTA KULFI

Ingredients

1 lt milk
100 gms khoa
50 gms pista and kesar
2 cups sugar
2 tbsps cornflour

Method

Boil the milk till it reduces to half its quantity. Add the cornflour mixed in a little water. Add the sugar and cook till the milk reduces to quarter of its original quantity. Add the khoa, pista, and kesars; stir well. Fill into kulfi moulds and chill. Before serving unmould.

20. BANBREAD PUDDING

Ingredients

- 4 slices bread
- 2 cups milk
- rind of ½ lemon
- 1 tbsp sugar
- 3 bananas, sliced into rounds
- 1 cup thick custard

Method

Break the bread into pieces. Boil the milk and pour over it. Allow the bread to soal till soft. Beat well. Stir the custard into it. Add the bananas and pour into a buttered dish. Add the grated rind. Sprinkle the sugar on top, and bake. Serve chilled.

21. PLUM PUDDING

Ingredients

- 115 gms maida
- 115 gms margarine
- 1 glass milk
- ½ tsp baking soda
- 115 gms currants
- 30 gms candied peel
- 115 gms brown sugar
- 115 gms grated carrots
- 115 gms breadcrumbs
- ½ tsp mixed spice powder
- 60 gms sultanas
- 60 gms raisins

Method

Soak the breadcrumbs in milk. Beat up and add all the dry ingredients. Mix well. Pour into a greased dish. Cover with greased paper, and steam for an hour. It can be preserved for a week. On the day it is to be served, again steam it on low flame for half an hour.

22. MANGO-BADAM PUDDING

Ingredients

4 ripe mangoes
1 lt milk
1 cup sugar
5 cardamoms, crushed
50 gms almonds, soaked
a few strands saffron

Method

Extract the mango pulp. Beat in a mixie and keep aside. Grind the badam with its skin. Add to the milk and bring it to a boil, strring so that the paste does not stick to the bottom. When the milk thickens, add the sugar. When the sugar dissolves, remove from the fine. Soak the saffron in a little milk and add to the milk. Add the cardamom, stir and cool. Add the beaten mango pulp, mix well and chill. Garnish with nuts or fruits.

23. CARROT PUDDING

Ingredients

¼ kg carrots, grated
1 cup sugar
1 tsp cardamom powder
nuts for decoration
½ lt milk
1 packet custard powder

Method

Cook the carrots in milk till soft. Puree when cool. Add the sugar and cook on slow fire for 10-15 minutes. Mix the custard powder with a little cold milk to form a smooth paste. Add to the boiling milk, stirring well. Remove from the fire and sprinkle cardamom powder. Chill and serve garnished with nuts.

24. CHOCOLATE ORANGINA

Ingredients

1 packet jelly (any flavour)
1 tin condensed milk
1 tbsp chocolate gratings
1 slab plain chocolate
½ cup cream
a few nuts

Method

Set the jelly as instructed on packet. Melt the chocolate and stir into the jelly. Whip the cream and condensed milk until very thick and fold into the semi-set jelly. Whip the cream until light and fluffy and just holds its shape. When the jelly has completely set, decorate it with the cream to cover the orangina completely. Place nuts on top with the chocolate gratings.

25. COFFEE MILK JELLY

Ingredients

4 cups milk
¼ cup sugar
1 tbsp gelatine
1 cup strong coffee
vanilla essence
1 tbsp warm water

Method

Heat 1 cup milk with coffee and half sugar till the sugar dissolves. Keep aside. In another pan, heat the remaining milk with sugar and vanilla till the sugar dissolves. Soak the gelatine in warm water and cook over low heat till it dissolves. Pour half of it into the coffee mixture and the other half into the vanilla mixture. Pour the vanilla mixture into a wet jelly mould and set in fridge. When half set, pour the coffee mixture over it and set. Serve chilled.

26. DOODHI MALAI

Ingredients

- 1 kg marrow (doodhi/lauki), grated
- a pinch of orange colour
- ½ tsp nutmeg powder
- 2 strands saffron, soaked in a little milk
- 1 packet gulab jamun mix
- 1 tbs ghee
- 1 lt milk
- 1 fistful long-grained rice
- ½ tsp cinnamon powder
- 1 tsp rose essence
- 2 cups sugar

Method

Squeze out the water from the marrow and spread the marrow on a paper towel to dry. Heat the ghee and saute the marrow till translucent. Stir the saffron into the narrow. Remove from the fire and cool. Boil the milk for a few minutes. Add the rice and cook till the milk reduces to half its quantity. Add the orange colour and remove from the fire. Add the cardamom, nutmeg and cinnamon powders and the essence. Cool. Make marble-size jamuns with the narrow and soak in sugar syrup. When well soaked, remove from the syrup. Add the syrup gradually to milk, stirring constantly. Toss the jamuns lightly into the marrow and spread out evenly in a casserole dish. Pour the milk all over the mixture gently. Garnish with nuts.

27. TRI-LAYER PUDDING

Ingredients

- 1 kg carrot, grated
- 200 gms sugar
- ½ lt milk
- 4 tsps nuts
- 1 kg bottlegoard, grated
- 50 gms custard powder
- 4 tsps ghee
- vanilla essence

Method

Heat half the ghee and fry the carrots. Cover and cook on low fire till tender. Add 50 gms sugar and stir till the mixture is dry. Likewise, repeat with the gourd. Make custard with sugar, vanilla and milk. Cool. Layer the bottom of a serving dish with custard, then carrots, again custard, then gourd followed by custard. Garnish with nuts.

28. RASPBERRY ICE-CREAM

Ingredients

1 lt milk
6 tbsps sugar
2 cups fresh cream
6 drops red colour
3 tbsps condensed milk
2 tsps raspberry essence

Method

Boil the milk till it reduces by half. Keep stirring constantly. Add the sugar and bring to a boil. Add the condensed milk and stir for five minutes. Remove from the fire. When cool, add the colour and essence and beat in a mixie for half a minute. Add the cream slowly, and heat again till the mixture is creamy. Freeze till mixture is slushy. Remove and beat again. Serve decorated with whipped cream and cherries.

29. APPLE CREAM

Ingredients

2 big apples
4 tbsps sugar
juices of ½ lemon
1 tsp vanilla essence
2½ cups milk
4 tbsps gelatine
a few pieces of apple (for decoration)

Method

Peel and chop the apples. Puree and add the lemon juice to it. Dissolve gelatine in a little hot water. Boil the milk and add the apple pulp and sugar to it. Cook for five minutes. Add the gelatine and remove form the fire. Ad the essence, stir well and chill till set. Before serving, pour the whipped cream and decorate with apple pieces.

30. PEACH DELIGHT

Ingredients

100 gms icing sugar
150 ml thick cream
½ cup chopped nuts
2 tsps rum
6 peaches, cut into halves
25 gms powdered sugar

Method

Place the peaches in a baking and serving bowl. Whip the cream over a bowl of ice cubes till thick and fluffy. Add the sugar gradually. Keep whipping till all the sugar has been used. Pour his over the peaches. Sprinkle the icing sugar over it. Add the rum, with a spoon to spread over the mixture. Preheat an oven, place the baking bowl in the owen, and bake till it begins to bubble. Remove and chill till serving time. Serve with custard sauce and nuts.

31. ORANGE JELLY

Ingredients

6 oranges
120 gms sugar
1 tbsp nuts (chopped)
160 ml water
1 tbsp gelatine
1½ cup cream

Method

Extract the juice from the oranges, and mix with the water and sugar. Heat the juice till the sugar dissolves. Soak the gelatine in lemon juice, and allow it to soften. Place it over a pan of hot water, and stir till the gelatine melts. Add the orange juice and mix well. Cool. Beat in cream and set in the fridge. Decorate with whipped cream chopped nuts.

32. MANGO MELODY

Ingredients

2 cups chopped mangoes
2 packets of jelly
¾ cup sugar
2 cups cottage cheese
1½ cups cream
4 cups hot water

Method

Set one packet of jelly as instructed. Chill till nearly set. Add the mango pieces and set completely. Blend the cottage cheese, cream and sugar in a mixie till smooth. Dissolve the other packet of jelly in 1 cup of water, and mix with the cheese puree, and blend again. Pour over the set jelly and chill. Serve chilled with whipped cream.

33. PAPAYA DELIGHT

Ingredients

10 peaches
1 tbsp lemon juice
¼ tsp nutmeg
1 tbsp honey
3 tbsps syrup
½ cup cream
2 tbsps arrowroot powder
¼ cup castor sugar

Method

Blend together the peaches, sugar, lemon juice, honey and nutmeg in a mixie to a smooth paste. Mix the arrrowroot powder with the syrup thoroughly. Add the peach mixture and cool on low flame, stirring constantly until the mixture turns glossy and thick. Remove from the fine and cool. Fold in the whipped cream gently, and pile in small stemmed glasses. Set in the fridge. Decorate with piped rosettes of whipped cream on top.

34. PINEAPPLE WONDER

Ingredients

½ tin pineapple
2 cups pineapple juice
3 tbsps gelatine
2 tsps pineapple essence
½ cup cream
50 gms cashew-raisins, chopped

Method

Dissolve the gelatine in ¼ cup of warm water. Mix the syrup from the tin with the pineapple juice and add the dissolved gelatine. Beat the ceam till thick. Beat the pineapple mixture till fluffy. Fold in the cream, pineapple pieces and essence. Allow to set. When half set, add the nuts into mixture. Set and serve chilled with pineapple sauce.

35. STRAWBERRY RIPPLE PUDDING

Ingredients

3 cups milk
1 cup sugar
2 tbsps powdered sugar
1 cup strawberries
1 tsp vanilla essence
3 tbsps custard powder
2 cups fresh cream
1 packet strawberry jelly
12 Marie biscuts

Method

Make custard with milk, custard powder and sugar. Mix the essence and allow to cool. Prepare the jelly as per instructions on the packet. Cut the strawberries into small pieces. Whip the cream with powdered sugar till stiff. Fold into the prepared custard. In a transparent bowl, spread the custard, and half of the semi-set jelly over it. Spread the biscuts over this. Cover with strawberry pieces, followed by the remaining jelly topping with the remaining custard. Spread whipped cream on top and decorate with some strawberry pieces. Serve chilled.

36. MANGO CREAMY JELLY

Ingredients

- 1 packet mango or banana jelly
- 1½ tbsps basmati rice, coarsely powdered
- 1 cup mango pieces
- ¼ cup sugar
- 2 cups milk
- ½ cup cream

Method

Heat the milk in a pan. Add the rice and cook till thick and creamy. Add the sugar and stir till it dissolves. Remove from the fire. Dissolve the jelly crystals in hot water. Cool. Add the mango pieces, cooked rice cream, and half of the fresh cream. Put in individual dishes and to set in the refrigerator. Decorate with cream and a few mango chunks.

SWEETS

SWEETS

1. COOKIE CRUMB DELIGHT

Ingredients

1 tin condensed milk
200 gms coconut biscuits, crushed
2 cups full cream milk
oil for greasing a thali

Method

Heat the milk in a thickss-bottomed pan. Gradually add condensed milk. Stirng continuously, so that they are well blended. Add the cookie crumbs a little at a time, stirring the mixture continuously. Cook on a low flame till it thickens. When it is soft, spread it on a greased thali. Flatten the mixture with the lack of a wooden spoon. Allow to cool, then place in the fridge for an hour till set. Cut into desired size or shape, and garnish with dry fruits. You can also place the mixture on an aluminium foil, cool, roll tightly and then place in fridge. Once set, cut into circles and serve.

2. GUJIA

Ingredients

60 gms maida
1 tbsp ghee

For the Filling

30 gms khoa
10 gms grated coconut
6 almonds, chopped
20 gms castor sugar
oil for frying
10 gms semolina, dry roasted
6 cashews, chopped
6 pista, chopped
100 gms sugar

Method

Add melted ghee to the maida and lightly mix with fingertips. Add water and knead to a stiff dough. Add the khoa with the semolina, coconut, nuts and castor sugar. Make six balls out of the dough and roll into small puris. Divide the filling into six portions. Place a portion of this in the centre of a puri. Fill all the other puris likewise. Moisten the edges with a little water, and fold each puri into half, pressing the edges together. Boil 25 ml water and dissolve the 100 gms sugar in it. When it comes to a two-string consistency, remove from the fire. Heat the oil for frying. Fry the gujias till golden brown. Strain the oil and soak in the sugar syrup for five minutes. Remove from the syrup and dry.

3. CHENNA MURKI

Ingredients

100 gms cottage cheese, cubed
¾ cup sugar
½ tsp cardamom powder
6 tbsps water
3 tbsps ghee
½ tsp lemon juice

Method

Heat the ghee and fry the cheese till golden brown. Drain well and cool. Mix the sugar and water and boil till the syrup thickens. Add the cardamom powder and remove from the heat. Add the lemon juice and cheese. Mix well so that the cheese pieces get well coated with sugar. Serve chilled.

4. GULAB JAMUN

Ingredients

- 1 cup khoa
- 1½ cups sugar
- ¼ tsp cardamom powder
- oil for frying
- 2 tbsps maida
- ¼ tsp baking powder
- 3 cups water

Method

Mix the sugar and water and boil till the syrup is thick. Remove form the fire and add the cardamom. Mix the khoa, flour, baking powder and water and knead into a soft and smooth dough. Make small balls of equal size. Heat the oil in a deep pan and fry the jamuns over medium heat until golden brown (or dark brown). Remove from the oil and immense in the sugar syrup. Serve hot or cold.

5. RASMALAI

Ingredients

- ½ lt milk
- 2 lemons
- 1 cup water
- 1 tsp maida
- 1 cup sugar
- ¼ tsp cardamom powder

For the Cream Sauce

- ¾ lt milk
- sliced almonds for garnishing
- 5 tbsps sugar

Method

Heat the milk for the rasmalai and bring it to a boil. Remove from the fire and squeeze the lemon juice into it. Strain the milk, and wash the paneer or 'chenna' under cold running water. Tie this in a muslin cloth and squeeze out the excess when water. Knead this with flour to a smooth dough. Make small balls of this, and keep aside. Mix sugar and water and boil it. Add the chenna balls and cook for 15 minutes with a lid partially covering pan. The chenna balls will bloat up. Cool and add the cardamom. For the cream sauce, boil the milk till it becomes thick and creamy (almost reducing to half its quantity). Add the rasmalais and decorate with the almond slices. Serve chilled.

6. CASHEWNUT BURFI

Ingredients

1½ cups cashewnuts
1 cup ghee
1 tsp cardamom powder
cup milk
2 cups sugar

Method

Soak the cashews in milk for an hour until soft. Grind to a smooth paste and blend with ghee and sugar. Cook on medium heat, stirring constantly until the mixture leaves the sides of the pan. Pour into a greased plate. Cool and cut into diamonds.

7. SANDESH

Ingredients

6 cups full-cream milk
1 tbsps chopped pistachios
½ tsp cardamom powder
juice of 2 lemons
1 tsp chopped almonds

Method

Boil the milk and add the lemon juice. When the milk curdles, strain and tie the chenna in a muslin cloth till all the water is drained. Remove from the cloth onto a pan. Mix in the sugar. Heat the pan and cook the chenna till it becomes a solid mass and all the water evaporates. Add the remaining and mix. Spread this on a greased dish. When cool, cut into the required shape.

8. PANEER ROLLS

Ingredients

1 lt milk
juice of 2 lemons
4 tbsps castor sugar
½ cup cream
chopped nuts for decoration

Method

Boil the milk and curdle it with the lemon juice. Strain and tie the chenna in a muslin cloth, hanging it for an hour to remove all the whey. Mix the almond powder with a little milk to make a smooth paste. Mix the chenna with half the sugar and form small balls. Roll the balls in the almond paste. Steam these over a pan of hot water for 10 minutes. Remove and cool. Mix the remaining sugar with cream, and roll the balls in it. Decorate with the nuts and chill.

9. MYSORE PAK

Ingredients

1 cup besan flour
2 cups sugar
2 cups ghee
½ cup water
1 tsp cardamom powder

Method

You can also used glaced cherries or candied peel for decoration to add colour to your sweet. Dry roast the flour until a fragrant smell emanates, and the colour is darker. In a heavy pan, melt the sugar in water and bring to a boil. Gradually add the flour, stirring constantly to avoid lumps forming. Add the ghee at intervals, stirring all the while. Continue stirring until the mixture leaves the sides and starts frothing. Pour into a greased rimmed plate. Before it hardens and sets, lightly mark into squares or rectangles. When cool and set, cut.

10. RASAGOLLA

Ingredients

6 cups milk
1 tsp semolina
2 cups sugar
a few strands of saffron
juice of 2 lemons
4 cups water
¼ tsp cardamom powder
rose essence (optional)

Method

Heat the milk and curdle it with the lemon juice. Tie in a muslin cloth and hang it till all the whey is strained. Mix this cheena with semolina, and knead until it is soft like butter. Make into balls and keep aside. Boil the sugar with water. Add the saffron and rose essence to make a thin syrup. Place the balls in syrup, and cook on very low heat until the balls become double their size and juicy. Remove the pan from the fire. Cool and chill.

11. JALEBI

Ingredients

2 cups maida
1 tbsp lemon juice
1 tsp cardamom powder
oil for frying
3 cups sugar
½ tsp orange or yellow colour
½ tsp saffron

Method

Mix flour with enough water to make a sticky pouring consistency ensuring there are no lumps. Beat well and leave covered for 24 hours. Boil 3 cups of water. Add the sugar and simmer till the syrup is sticky. Add the lemon juice. Remove the scum from the top of the sugar with a spoon. Add the warmed, crushed saffron, colour and cardamom powder. Keep aside. Heat the oil in a wide, deep pan. when it is very hot, lower the heat. Beat the overnight batter and pipe it through a smooth coconut shell hole into the hot oil in a circular motion making four or five circles for each jilebi. Fry till just crisp and turn over. Remove and dip in the syrup for five minutes. Remove from the syrup and arrange in a platter.

12. CHURMA LADDOOS

Ingredients

2 cups green gram flour
3 cups sugar
½ cup raisins
½ tsp saffron
oil for frying
2 tbsps ghee
½ cup milk
1 tsp cardamom powder
1 tbsp almonds, chopped

Method

Mix the flour with the ghee. Add the milk (and water, if necessary) to make a medium-consistency batter. Boil the sugar with 2 cups of water and simmer till the syrup is of three-thread consistency. Keep aside. Heat the oil till hot. Through a colander with fairly medium-sized holes, drop the batter into the oil. Fry the boondis till golden and crisp. Remove from the oil and immerse them in the syrup. When all the batter has been used up and boondis fried and soaked in syrup, add the raisins, nuts and saffron to the boondis. While warm, make laddoos with greased palms.

13. SHAKKARPARA

Ingredients

1 cup maida
2 tbsps sesame
pinch of soda bicarb
oil for deep frying
1 cup sugar
½ tsp cardamom powder
a few drops of rose essence

Method

Mix together the maida, baking powder, sesame and cardamom powder. Add enough water to make into a stiff dough. Roll into a thin round. Cut into strips. Cup each strip into diamond shape. Make a syrup of one-thread consistency with 1 cup sugar. Add the rose essence. In hot oil fry the shakkarparas and drop them into the hot syrup. After half a minute, remove from the syrup and dry them. Cool and store in airtight tins.

14. MANGO DELIGHT

Ingredients

1 cup khoa
1 cup mango pulp
1 tbsp cornflour
½ tsp cardamom powder
½ cup sugar
1 cup paneer, crumbled
½ tsp saffron

Method

Add ½ cup water to sugar, and cook till the syrup has one-thread consistency. Add the paneer and khoa. Mix the mango and cornflour smoothly, and add to the paneer-khoa. Then add the saffron and cardamom powder. Cook over a gentle flame till the mixture dries, and pour into a greased plate, evening the surface. Cool thoroughly and then cut into squares.

15. LAVANG LATIKA

Ingredients

- 2 cups maida
- 1 tsp whole cloves
- ½ tsp cardamom powder
- ½ tsp nutmeg powder
- 2 tbsps nuts and raisins chopped
- ½ tsp lemon juice
- ¾ cup khoa
- ¾ cup grated copra
- 1 cup sugar
- oil for deep frying

Method

Mix the khoa, copra, 3 tbsps sugar, and cook till blended. Add the nuts nutmeg and cardamom powders. Mix well. Knead a stiff dough with flour and 4 tbsps oil. Make a syrup with the remaining sugar and water of one-string consistency. Add the lemon juice. Make equal portions of the dough and khoa. Roll out the dough. Place the khoa in the centre and fold over from four sides, fixing the end with a clove. Make similar lavang latikas with the dough and khoa. Heat the oil and fry the lavang latikas till golden. Drain and dip in the sugar syrup. Dry and serve chilled.

16. BESAN LADDOOS

Ingredients

- 2 cups besan flour
- 1 cups ghee
- 2 tbsps crushed nuts
- 2 cups powdered sugar
- 1 tsp cardamom powder

Method

Roast the gram flour in a tablespoon of ghee till a nice aroma emerges, on a low flame. Remove and cool for a while. Mix the flour and sugar, adding the melted ghee. Add the cardamom powder and the nuts. Mix thoroughly and make into small balls. Cool and serve.